Praise for *Orphan Justice*

Johnny ushers us into honest self-assessment, often re-aligning our paradigms. *Orphan Justice* will make you laugh, smile, cry, squirm, . . . and ultimately be stirred to effective action as we advocate for the vulnerable.

> Andy Lehman, vice president, Lifesong for Orphans

Johnny takes off the kid gloves and passionately calls the church to rediscover the mandate to care for the widow and the orphan. Be prepared to travel with him into places of poverty and brokenness, but be inspired by glimpses of hope. Read this book and catch a vision for the unique role you can play in ensuring every child has a home.

> Peter Greer, president and CEO, HOPE International and author of *The Poor Will Be Glad* and *The Spiritual Danger of Doing Good*

While every Christian is not called to adopt children, every Christian should be involved somehow in caring for orphans in their affliction. Because of this, I rejoice to see this book by Johnny Carr, who understands the global orphan crisis on a personal, professional, and evangelical level. His research, stories, biblical rational, and practical exhortations are both enlightening and enlivening. I love the end of the chapters "What You Can Do." Here is a book that would change lives, churches, and the world if we would implement it.

> Tony Merida, Southeastern Baptist Theological Seminary

Are you considering adoption? Read this book! Perhaps adoption isn't for you—read this book anyway! There are many different ways you can and should be involved in the important work of orphan care worldwide. *Orphan Justice* will equip you to embrace God's call to "look after orphans and widows in their distress and to keep oneself from being polluted by the world."

> Jim Daly, president, Focus on the Family

Orphan Justice is a fast-paced, hard-hitting book that will anger and inspire you to rethink your view of orphans, the gospel, and how the church should respond by tackling issues that most want to ignore or avoid. This book will prompt you and your church to take action and to tangibly care for the fatherless with wisdom, tenacity, and intelligence.

> Chris Marlow, founder and CEO, Help One Now

Johnny Carr does not write about justice for the orphan as one who merely observes from a distance, but as one whose life's journey, whose life's mission is to bring justice to the orphan. There is no leader in the evangelical orphan care movement whose work I value more. *Orphan Justice* is full of fearless thinking that is compelled by the love of Jesus. Johnny loves the orphans of our world because Jesus first loved him. Read. Be empowered. And then pursue justice for the orphan.

—Dan Cruver, founder of Together for Adoption and author of *Reclaiming Adoption*

It's been heartening to see the church get excited about orphan care, but sometimes the best of intentions do not always align with best practice. *Orphan Justice* is a book that bridges the gap between passion and practice. Johnny Carr tackles the tough issues involved in orphan care, from the realities of institutionalization to the racism that still permeates our society. It's an important read for church leaders, advocates, and anyone interested in answering the call to care for orphans.

Kristen Howerton, blogger, Rage Against the Minivan

If you're seeking a book to make you feel good about yourself, try the self-help section. But if you're looking for a personal, provocative, and sometimes raw challenge to see the world in fresh ways, *Orphan Justice* is a must-read. Using gripping stories and surprising Scriptures, Johnny Carr shakes readers from their slumber and alerts them to a global crisis begging for our attention. Warning: Do not read this book unless you're prepared to be changed!

Jonathan Merritt, author of *A Faith of Our Own: Following Jesus Beyond the Culture Wars*

No one has stood more at the forefront of the evangelical orphan care movement than Johnny Carr. In this provocative book, Carr reminds us that while orphan care is never about less than adoption, orphan care is about an entire range of issues. Carr prophetically calls the church to care for orphans by combatting racism, trafficking, poverty, and abortion. Even when you don't agree with all Carr's answers, you will be blessed by wrestling with him through the questions.

Russell D. Moore, dean, Southern Baptist Theological Seminary and author of *Adopted for Life*

Johnny Carr is changing the conversation on the orphan crisis. I laughed, cried, and winced in anger as Johnny shared stories from his personal and professional mission to care for the least of us. In *Orphan Justice*, Johnny brings us into a messy conversation and shows us practical solutions that can build consensus to move the needle.

Ken Coleman, talk radio host of The Ken Coleman Show and author of *One Question: Life-Changing Answers from Today's Leading Voices*

Orphan Justice provokes the reader to action. The statistics and realities contained within can cause one of three responses. Either it can paralyze us to the point of complacency or it can energize us for a season to do as much as possible with the need becoming our motivation. Ultimately, however, it is Johnny's heart that a third option would be chosen: That the worldwide church would awaken and be driven to seek the face of the Father as we serve the fatherless. It is so Christ-exalting to wrestle with this content and be motivated, not by the need, but by the gospel. This book is both compelling and heartfelt and worth your investment of time.

Herbert M. Newell IV, president/executive director, Lifeline Children's Services, Inc.

Orphan Justice explores the big picture of what orphan care can and should look like. Not all of us are called to the same ministry, but all of us must do something. This book is eye-opening and important, a call to action written with incredible grace. It's a must-read for the church and for all people wanting to do "orphan care" well and responsibly.

Katie Davis, author of *Kisses from Katie*

Many of us have a desire to help orphans, but we don't know where to start. *Orphan Justice* gives the VISION we need to understand how we, as the church, can be a part of the solution to the orphan care crisis. There's a role for everyone to play.

Mac Powell, lead singer, Third Day

Johnny Carr has written such an important and essential book on why we should all be called to help orphaned children. Yes, it is heartbreaking to think about the millions of children around the world who are hurting and forgotten, but Romans 8 reminds us so clearly that if we want to share in God's blessings, we have to share in His suffering as well. There are so many real and tangible ways to get involved in making a difference, and while not everyone is called to adopt, everyone CAN get involved through volunteering, or sponsoring, or being a voice for those who live as orphans. This book calls all church members to turn their faith into action so that every child growing up in an orphanage will someday know their lives matter.

> Amy Eldridge, chief executive officer, Love Without Boundaries Foundation, "Hope and Healing for Orphaned Children"

The theme of caring for the orphans and the fatherless permeates the biblical narrative and puts the gospel on display. Johnny Carr writes a compelling, scripturally sound account of why caring for orphans should be as normal in the life of God's people as things like weekly fellowship or prayer. If you want your church to get excited about the practical possibilities of applying the gospel to suffering children locally and around the world, get *Orphan Justice* in their hands. It will light a fire for mission.

> Anthony Bradley, Ph.D., Associate Professor of Theology and Ethics, The King's College and author of *Liberating Black Theology*

Johnny's powerful life-narrative and insights based on years of experience offer readers an approachable look at the complex social issues facing our world. Each issue the book addresses is coupled with practical ways you can engage to make a difference. I encourage anyone looking to move past the "religious fad" of social justice and towards real change to read this book.

> Jason Locy, author of *Veneer: Living Deeply in a Surface Society* and adoptive dad

Johnny Carr has played a major role in helping Catalyst understand adoption is an issue for Christian leaders. Through *Orphan Justice*, he is now challenging each of us to not only continue in our important work of seeing orphaned children placed in families, but also to leave our comfort zones and minister to orphaned children in all areas of their lives. The combination of Johnny's story and his practical suggestions will move you to action.

> Brad Lomenick, CEO, Catalyst

orphanjustice

Johnny Carr

WITH LAURA CAPTARI

orphanjustice

How to Care for Orphans Beyond Adopting

social justice   aids   foster care   abortion

man trafficking   hunger   poverty

social justice   homelessness   racism

B&H
PUBLISHING GROUP
Nashville, Tennessee

Dedication

To Beth: "This is all your fault." Your heart was in tune with God's Spirit, and you never gave up on the dream He gave you. I dedicate this book to you and to each of our children—Heather, Jared, James, Xiaoli, and JJ.

—Johnny

To Dorin: I still can't believe God brought you around the world to me! Your love and support have been my fuel when I was ready to give up writing. May our family one day picture the church "from every tribe, nation, people, and language."

—Laura

Table of Contents

Acknowledgments

The content of this book is "way over my head." I'll be the first to tell you that I could never have completed this project alone. As God birthed a passion in me, I reached out to many people for help, advice, and feedback on each of the chapters. Words fall short to express how grateful I am to the team God brought into my life. Looking back now, I see God's hand so clearly in every step of this project.

Orphan Justice would still be a dream if not for the encouragement of two main people—my wife, Beth, and my boss, Marc Andreas. Beth, I really don't know how to even put this into words. Your support and love is more than I have ever deserved. Marc, you are the best boss I have ever had the privilege of working with. I thank you for the encouragement and challenge to write.

I also want to thank Bethany Christian Services' CEO, Bill Blacquire, for encouraging me along the way. Additional thanks goes to all of my colleagues at Bethany who have taught me so much over the last several years, but especially the following people who personally contributed by reviewing sections of the book: Dr. Dennis Feaster, Pamela Harrington, Tendai Masiriri, Sara Ruiter, Trish Small, Kristine Faasse, Sandra McLaughlin, and Marlene Hibma.

I can't thank you enough, Matt Towles, for introducing me to Laura Faidley. After our first meeting, I knew without a doubt, Laura, that you were the right person to partner with to "fix" all my mistakes, help with the research, add your thoughts and content, and make me sound good. What an honor to see you and Dorin join your lives together during this process and have the name Captari on the cover of this book. You have been professional, honest, and a joy to work with. Thanks for sharing part of your life with us.

Through another good friend and colleague, I was introduced to Curtis Yates. More than an agent, you have become a friend. Your wisdom and experience have been invaluable. I am so thankful for how you and Karen have embraced this project and that you live the message of this book.

The same goes to Jedidiah Coppenger, Amanda Sloan, and Shannon Kozee at B&H Publishing. Thank you for walking this journey with me and for believing in this book.

To our friend "Hannah," who serves as headmistress of the Deaf School in China. You have inspired our family in ways you will never know. You are incredibly brave, and I pray that your life is honored in this book.

God has blessed me with the best friends in the world. Two in particular have been extremely helpful—Jonathan Merritt, author and speaker, and Jedd Medefind of Christian Alliance for Orphans. Jonathan, thank you for teaching me how to write. Jedd, thank you for challenging me on the content and for your wise counsel.

Thank you, Chris Mabry, for your encouragement, friendship, and for providing a quiet and inspiring place to write.

To my colleagues and friends who agreed to read various chapters with a critical eye and a red pen, I am so grateful for each of you. Thank you for sharing your wisdom and investing your time to help bring this book to life—Elizabeth Styffe of Saddleback Church, Kelly Rosati of Focus on the Family, Dr. Tony Merida of Southern Baptist Theological Seminary, Dr. Matthew Towles and Josh Brown of Liberty University, Dr. Anthony Bradley of Kings College, Dan Cruver of Together for Adoption, Herbie Newell of Lifeline Adoption Services, Peter Greer of HOPE International, Turk and Beth Holt of Heavenbound Ministries, Lee Kricher of Pittsburgh East Community Church, Tom Lukasik of 4KIDS of South Florida, Vernon Pierre of Roosevelt Community Church, Lonnie Wesley of Greater Little Rock Baptist Church, Dr. Leo Day of Olive Baptist Church, Jason Locy of FiveStone, Noel Dear of First Baptist Church of Heath, Dr. Willy Rice of Calvary Baptist Church, Jeff Howard of Heritage Baptist Church, and Carl Weiser of Hyland Heights Baptist Church. Also thank you to some great friends: Christopher Matyjasik, Rich Santo, Wanda Wang, Dexter Tolbert, Mary Waters, and Shane "George" Lambert.

Saying thank you to each of these friends and listing their names does not necessarily suggest their endorsement on this book. However, their feedback was critical in the writing and editing process.

To my mom and dad, Barbara and John Carr, my sisters, Debbie and Pam, and Beth's brother Bryan and wife, Jenifer, thank you for welcoming our children into our family without regard to skin color or disability.

To Milton and Patricia Parris, you would be so proud of Beth. We miss you both.

Most of all, to my loving, kind, patient, and forgiving God. May You get all the glory and use this story to change hearts and move other Christ followers to action. Ultimately, Jesus, this is Your book . . . Your story . . . that You are working out in me day by day.

To my Abba Father, thank You for adopting me as Your son and for bringing me into Your family.

Introduction

Imagine children lined up shoulder to shoulder all the way around the earth's equator. Now consider that all of the orphaned kids in the world would not fit in that line. There are too many of them. According to UNICEF, 153 million kids worldwide have lost one or both parents due to all causes.[1] That's twice the total number of children in the U.S.[2]

You may think I am here to tell you that American Christians need to step up and adopt all of these orphaned children. I am not. I believe adoption is a great ministry; in fact, I have three adopted kids of my own. However, not all of these 153 million kids can—or need to—be adopted. But they do need our help. And we must give that help, because orphaned and vulnerable children have no other hope or future. More importantly, by obeying God to care for the fatherless, we have the opportunity to experience Him in ways we never imagined.

James 1:27 says, "Pure and genuine religion in the sight of God the Father means caring for orphans and widows in their distress and refusing to let the world corrupt you" (NLT). Though it did not come easily or naturally to me, I have learned to care deeply for orphans over the past several years. On September 5, 2005, we adopted our son, James, and he has changed our everything. As a result of finding our son, we have all found so much more—this little boy has found a life and our family has found the pure religion spoken of in James 1:27.

I invite you to join me on a journey as we get to the heart of what God desires for every one of the 153 million orphaned and vulnerable children around the world. It's not just a statistic. We are talking about real children—children whom God our Father loves and longs to rescue. Deuteronomy 10:18 tells us, "[God] ensures that orphans and widows receive justice" (NLT), and Psalm 68:5 tells us He is "a father of the fatherless." Yes, God fights for orphans and loves them as their Father, but His Word also exhorts *us* to "defend the cause of orphans" (Isa. 1:17 NLT).

In this book, you will discover the problems that go hand in hand with the orphaned children of our world—human trafficking, AIDS, poverty, and more. We must do all we can to alleviate and eradicate these problems. We cannot settle for cheap solutions because we as Christ followers have a responsibility before God to act and, more importantly, to *keep* acting. We cannot be silent while children around the world are being robbed of hope and life.

My Challenges to You

If you are like most people, you read a book—or parts of it—and then put it on a shelf and forget about it. However, the purpose of this book is not for it to be read, but for those who read it to be changed. To do something to make a difference in the lives of orphaned and vulnerable children around the world. With that in mind, I want to offer you several challenges as you read.

First, I encourage you to ask someone to read the book with you. Discuss it together at the end of each chapter or as part of a small group. I have found that if I talk about what I have read with others, I often gain a fresh perspective and find that I missed insights that others caught. Discussion also helps us flesh out some of our own thoughts and areas of agreement or disagreement with these complex issues. This book is not designed or meant to resolve all of the problems related to orphaned and vulnerable children. It is meant to lead you to think, pray, and hopefully act.

The second challenge is to choose at least one action step you can take from each chapter and implement it within the next year. You will discover many ideas throughout these pages, and at the end of each chapter, under the "What You Can Do" section, you will find even more suggestions for how to help in three different levels of involvement. The first level includes areas where anyone can serve. These activities will require very little commitment. The second type of action step will describe steps many people can take, though these will require some commitment. Finally, the third level of engagement will suggest a lifestyle change that a few people can do. These tasks will require a lot of commitment, and are not feasible in some cases. As you prayerfully consider these options, remember that each level is just as important as the others. How you choose to become involved may be influenced by a number of factors, including your stage of life, the amount of time you can feasibly commit, the resources you have available, the leading of the Holy Spirit, and even your locale.

I also challenge you to get your children involved in orphan care. As you read, think about ways you can paint a vision for your kids to reach out and help children in need around the world. As a family, brainstorm ways that you can get involved, invest sacrificially, and make a difference in other kids' lives. Challenge *your children* to do more than care about themselves, your biological family, and the things that make them comfortable.

Finally, I want to challenge you to commit to having an open mind as you read. If I had picked up this book six years ago, I would have responded with a defensive, critical attitude. I probably would not have read more than a chapter or two. My prayer is that as you read, the Holy Spirit will move you out of your comfort zone and into a place of gut-honest heart examination. Please know that I am writing from a broken spirit, not an accusatory spirit. My desire is to share with you what the Lord has taught me, starting with this truth: We can't say that we love orphans while failing to address the social ills that directly affect their lives.

**For more orphan care resources,
visit www.orphanjusticethebook.com.**

CHAPTER 1

True Religion
Orphans and My Family

Motionless bodies met my gaze as I stepped into the courtyard. James tensed up in my arms and clung desperately to my neck as I stood there in shock, trying to grasp the inescapable reality of this place he called home. The nearly two-dozen orphans with special needs in front of me were confined to crude high chairs. Flies were buzzing around pans positioned underneath each chair. A closer examination revealed why. The pans were full of excrement. James's eyes, full of fear, stared into mine and pleaded silently, "Please don't leave me here!"

Though the physical conditions were horrifying, that is not what haunts me the most about that day. It was the children's blank gazes. We were the first non-Asian people the children in this Chinese orphanage had ever seen, yet they didn't point, laugh, or even stare at us. They just sat there, some with their heads down on the trays and others simply staring aimlessly into space.

My wife, Beth, and I had traveled to Zhenshi,[1] China, to adopt our son from this orphanage. Guo Ya Zhou was brought to our hotel room the day before. I had quickly scooped up the precious four-year-old deaf orphan, and he had barely let go of me since.

5

The entire event was scary for all of us, but I was filled with love for our new son, who we renamed James Ze Carr. We had been told that Ze is the Chinese word for "chosen." He had been chosen by his heavenly Father and given to us as a gift. I can't fully express in words how it felt to play a part in his redemption.

The next day we were standing in the horrifying conditions of James's orphanage in one of the poorest cities in Asia, as already described. Malnutrition and disease ravaged the small bodies of the children in the courtyard. Since James is deaf, I couldn't comfort him with my voice or tell him we wouldn't leave him there. I simply held him securely against my chest so that he would feel safe, yet James began to scream and cry uncontrollably.

Once inside the compound, Beth and I witnessed things that shocked us. I tensed up, much like James had done in the courtyard. Infants were starving. Children were dying from both major and minor medical issues. It was evident that the workers truly loved the children, but they were barely surviving themselves, and didn't have the necessary resources to properly care for the children.

Standing in that orphanage, little did I know the radical changes that would take place in my life. Humbled and broken, I walked away a different man.

God, Football, and the American Dream

I was not always open to adoption. I grew up in a conservative Christian home in the South, and we were more focused on following the rules—no drinking, no smoking, no dancing—than on social justice issues.

Growing up in Alabama, you learn to love two things from birth: God and football (and not in that order). When it came to football, I was an Auburn fan—the only one of "that kind" in my family. In the religious department, I was for Jesus. Everybody was. I didn't know anyone who wasn't a "Christian." Although for many people going to church was optional, praying before a football game was not. Band members removed their fancy hats with tall feathers. Ball players took off their helmets. Fans held their caps in hand. Even the kids playing cup football on the side of the stadium scolded each other if their game accidentally continued while the cheerleader prayed over the PA system.

I was evangelical, conservative, and proud of it. I followed the rules and shared the gospel. Most of the people in our church were trained in Evangelism Explosion and went out witnessing door-to-door at least one night a week. We were good at keeping ourselves unspotted from the world and sharing our personal witness, but in all of our passion for the gospel, we neglected to place the same importance on caring for those in distress, as we are commanded to do in Scripture.

Every time I heard about missionaries digging clean wells, working with HIV/AIDS patients, or trying to alleviate poverty, I rolled my eyes. *Why are they wasting their time?* I thought. *Don't they know that the gospel is what really counts?*

To be honest, I took a great deal of pride in the fact that I was right and they were wrong—*they* being anyone who didn't agree with me theologically. I was especially contemptuous toward anyone who had fallen prey to the liberal "social gospel," the trend in Christian circles where people were passionate about meeting people's physical and emotional needs while neglecting to share the gospel. I often criticized my liberal colleagues. *They've missed the heart of the gospel,* I thought. *One day, maybe they'll wake up and see the truth before they waste their entire lives doing humanitarian work.*

But now, as I look back, I see how narrow-minded I was. I seemed to frame everything in terms of either/or, all or nothing—either verbally sharing the gospel OR meeting people's physical needs. I didn't realize I was missing the true meaning of religion—one that includes BOTH sharing the gospel and meeting people's physical needs.

Then I met Beth, the sign language interpreter at our Baptist campus ministry in northern Alabama. The first time I saw Beth, she was signing for Heather Whitestone, who would later become the first Miss America with a disability. I barely noticed Miss America, though; Beth was the one who caught my eye.

I finally mustered the courage to ask Beth out. In one of our early conversations, she shared with me how she ached to adopt a deaf child. Without thinking too much about it, I responded, "Wow. That would be a great thing to do." What I didn't tell Beth was that adoption was out of the question for me, *especially* adopting a child with a disability. Sign language was cute for college girls, but definitely not for me. After all, I wanted to laugh, roughhouse, and play football with my little boys. I wanted to talk with them about the latest baseball trade or which NFL teams would make the playoffs, not sit and contort my fingers into weird shapes.

A year later, the sign language interpreter walked down the aisle to be my wife, and I could not have been happier. I had dismissed adoption as nothing more than Beth's college dream, particularly when our daughter Heather was born. I was such a proud dad. She was perfect with her little pinched red face, a startlingly loud scream, and big brown eyes. Four years later, along came Jared, and I thought that our family was complete.

I had the American dream—a beautiful and educated wife, two great kids, a fantastic job, two cars, and a house in a neighborhood with restrictive covenants. The only thing we were missing was the white picket fence because those stupid covenants wouldn't allow it.

How God Broke Through

I started working in church ministry when I was twenty-three years old, and by the time I graduated from Liberty Baptist Theological Seminary in 2001, I was steadily climbing the Christian ministry ladder one rung—one church—at a time.

At Jerry Falwell's university, I was able to spend time with him and learn from the best of the best in conservative evangelicalism . . . and I was determined I would *be* the best. Swept up in not only the American dream but also the "Christian dream," I dreamed big about how God would use *me* (big emphasis on me). As the churches where I ministered grew, my head grew, and my family was along for the ride. Every congregation I served was a little bit bigger and offered a little nicer perks than the previous one. In 2004, I took a position as Pastor of Ministry and Leadership Development at one of the fastest growing churches in the Florida panhandle.

While on the job, I met with a visiting missionary who wouldn't stop talking about a deaf orphanage in Belarus. I didn't have any idea where in the world Belarus was, and I had zero interest in deaf orphans, but I was a pastor, so I knew I had to at least seem interested in what this missionary was saying. Apparently the orphans needed loving, Christian families to adopt them. As the words "that would be a great thing to do" came out of my mouth, I remembered that I had spoken the same sentence to my wife many years earlier, before we had "moved past" the adoption thing.

A month after that meeting, Beth and I were having another conversation about adoption, much like the one we had while we were dating. But this time I didn't pull the "that would be great" card and tune her out. I actually listened. Hearing my wife's deep desire to welcome a deaf orphan into our home struck me like it never had before. I began to see my selfishness and arrogance. God was chipping away at my American dream, and I finally promised to call and get some information about the adoption process.

I did an Internet search for "Belarus international adoption" and picked up the phone to call the first hit—Nightlight Adoption Agency. I was somewhat relieved to find out that Belarus was closed to international adoptions. *Well, I guess God is closing that door.* I was just about to hang up when Ron, the guy on the other end of the line, asked me a strange question: "What specifics are you looking for in an adoption?" I stumbled over my words, but managed to tell him we were looking for a child under the age of six, deaf, and with no other disabilities. Then we hung up.

Ten minutes later, the phone rang again. It was Ron. "Check your e-mail," he told me. I opened a picture of a four-year-old Chinese boy and just stared. *Could this be my son?* I thought. *He doesn't look like me—but he needs somebody to call Dad. He needs somebody to call him son.*

Exactly seven months later, Beth and I were in China, along with Heather and Jared, getting ready to meet our new son. You've already read about how God gave James to us. But that's not the end of the story.

In the process of James's adoption, Beth came across an adorable picture online of a little Chinese girl sitting on a footstool, sticking her tongue out. A family who had adopted a child from an orphanage two hours from James's city had snapped the photo. The caption read, "I tried to whisper 'Jesu aye ni' to her, which is 'Jesus loves you' in Chinese, but the orphanage worker told me that she was deaf and couldn't hear anything."

My wife immediately called Heather into the computer room. A few seconds later I heard, *"Johnny?!"* It was that all-too-familiar tone that communicates, "Honey, I really want something and you are going to think that I am crazy for asking but I am going to sound so sweet that you will not be able to resist it."

Beth was beaming as she spoke, "Look at this little girl. She is four years old, in the same province where James is from, and she's deaf! She really needs a family!" I would love to say that I responded with a very spiritual answer, but I didn't. I balked. The amazing thing is that even in my doubt, God worked. In May of 2007, we found ourselves back in China adopting Xiaoli (Shao-lee).

During the twenty-six-hour flight home from China after adopting Xiaoli, all I could think about were the starving, desperate, and forgotten children in the deplorable orphanages James and Xiaoli had been rescued from. A question kept running through my head: *If what I've seen in these orphanages is real, do I care enough to do more than adopt two kids?*

It continued to plague me as I returned to my American dream life. I suddenly realized I didn't need the white picket fence or the sleek Honda. As I stood in line at Starbucks for a five-dollar latte or ordered a twenty-dollar steak at a restaurant, I was struck by the difference between my life and that of the orphans back in China and around the world. Sitting behind my big desk as Pastor of Ministry and Leadership Development, I wondered what that title really meant. Did I have a responsibility toward the orphans of the world, beyond James and Xiaoli?

I began to study Scripture like never before, discovering God's great love and concern for the fatherless. Verses about orphans that I had never noticed jumped off the page, and the one that stuck out the most was James 1:27, which I've already mentioned: "Pure and genuine religion in the sight of God the Father means caring for orphans and widows in their distress and refusing to let the world corrupt you" (NLT).

In our Western church culture, we tend to view religion as a negative thing. It is no surprise that the YouTube video titled "Why I Hate Religion, But Love Jesus" went viral. However, James offers us the meaning of true religion—caring for orphans and widows in their time of need and keeping ourselves unstained from the world. We frequently focus on keeping ourselves unstained, but we often fail in the area of taking care of orphans and widows.

The Grim Reality

We live in a fallen world. War, famine, and disease ensure that there will always be orphans among us. Every day, children are orphaned or abandoned due to economic need or disabilities. Understanding the plight of orphans and their families is critical.

In many cultures, mystic beliefs lead people to assume that a child born with a disability is possessed by an evil spirit or is the direct result of a curse. Families believe they must dispose of the child to free themselves from the curse. In other cases, families know that they will not have the resources to take care of the child, especially in the case of a disability. The sad reality is that many parents believe that their child will have a better life in an orphanage.

James and Xiaoli were both born deaf. Their parents probably could not confirm that they were deaf until they were about two or three years old. James was abandoned at a bus station, and Xiaoli was abandoned at a grocery store. Surprisingly, these were actually very safe places to leave the children because they were public locations. The toddlers were noticed, law enforcement was notified, and the children were delivered to an orphanage. My children's birth parents were most likely not cruel, but probably felt very desperate. They likely were hoping for the best for their kids. If they had wanted to be cruel, these parents would have left their toddlers in an abandoned field or drowned them in a river. This practice, known as infanticide, is common in many cultures.[2] James and Xiaoli's parents actually took a huge risk by leaving their children in crowded places, because someone could have caught them in the act. Punishment would have been swift and severe. This does not excuse their behavior; it simply serves to show that these parents were not intending cruelty toward their children.

It is hard for me to understand abandonment as a sacrificial, merciful act. But as I have talked with Christian leaders around the world and as I have walked through the process of adopting my children, I have developed a new understanding of the desperation that hopelessness brings. I am still unable to fathom abandoning my child, and it does not change the fact that such behavior is wrong, but my eyes have been opened.

Parents who abandon their children are often unable to provide for basic physical needs and hope that an orphanage will be able to help. But more than just food and shelter, *these children need a family.* As Christ followers, we have a responsibility to do something . . . and most of us need to consider doing something more than just writing a check. We must humble ourselves to consider where we have been wrong—where we have disobeyed God's Word and neglected to care for orphaned and vulnerable children.

I explained in the introduction that UNICEF has estimated that there are 153 million orphaned children worldwide. It is important to note that while most of us think of an orphan as a child who has lost both parents, these children are actually called "double orphans." Children with only one living parent are called "single orphans." Many children lose one parent through war, famine, or disease. Two-thirds of the time, kids lose their fathers first. Though they technically still have one parent, these single orphans are extremely vulnerable to disease, poverty, abuse, and other social ills and stigmas. Many of these children end up in orphanages, living with other family members, or living with an entirely different family even though they have a living parent. Most sources agree that there are approximately 18 million double orphans worldwide.

Research about orphans shows that "more often than not, the neediest children are sick, disabled, traumatized, or older than five."[3] These children are susceptible to poverty, HIV/AIDS, human trafficking, being stuck in an orphanage for their entire childhood, and many other issues that we will explore at length in this book.

Lest we think that orphans only exist in other countries, we must also look at our own problems. Here in the United States, there are nearly 400,000 children in the foster care system at any given time, and some of those foster homes are not exactly ideal. In addition, more than 100,000 of those children are waiting to be adopted.[4]

The numbers can be confusing, and knowing how to minister to these children's needs can be difficult. Some need family reunification, sponsorship, education, or medical assistance. Others need a temporary family to live with or permanency through adoption. All of the 153 million children worldwide do not need to be adopted. "It is very difficult to identify exactly how many orphaned children do not have families or will never be able to return to their family if the family is still alive or accessible," says Bill J. Blacquiere, CEO of Bethany Christian Services and a thirty-year veteran of advocacy for orphaned and vulnerable children. "Although we don't have a clear estimate of the number that need to be adopted, the numbers are in the millions, not the thousands."[5]

For the purposes of this book, we will refer to the UNICEF estimate of 153 million children who are *orphaned* and *vulnerable*. Some of these children need adoptive families. Others need support so their families can keep them out of an orphanage. All of these children have physical, emotional, and/or spiritual needs. They face a host of challenges. In the midst of their desperation, they cry out for hope. And our redeemer God longs for His people to be on the front lines of providing compassion, support, and gospel-centered care.

God's Heart for Orphans

I see time and again that caring for orphaned and vulnerable children is not often on the radar screen for many Christians. Somehow, in our concern for living a "good Christian life," many of us are missing God's passion for the fatherless.

Yet, caring for the needy is one of the main purposes of the church. Throughout Scripture, it is easy to see that God has a special place in His heart for the fatherless, the widow, and the alien. This is a rebuke and a wake-up call to us. Scripture is not silent on the issue of orphan care. Throughout the Old Testament, "orphans" and "the fatherless" are mentioned forty-one times. In Old Testament law, many specific guidelines are given for interacting with orphans. As you read the following verses, look for God's heart.

- "He executes justice for the fatherless and the widow, and loves the foreigner, giving him food and clothing" (Deut. 10:18).

- "Do not deny justice to a foreigner or fatherless child" (Deut. 24:17).
- "When you reap the harvest in your field, and you forget a sheaf in the field, do not go back to get it. It is to be left for the foreigner, the fatherless, and the widow, so that the LORD your God may bless you in all the work of your hands" (Deut. 24:19).

Caring for the marginalized of society—widows, orphans, and foreigners—lies at the heart of Yahweh's covenant with His people. These verses speak blatantly about the role of God's people in caring for the fatherless and inviting them into community. It seems apparent that in Old Testament culture, orphans lived as part of the community and were cared for by God's people.

Scripture doesn't spell out a detailed strategy for orphan care, but God does speak directly to the role of His people. In fact, God promises judgment on those who do not take care of the weak and needy: "Cursed is anyone who denies justice to foreigners, orphans, or widows" (Deut. 27:19 NLT).

To our God, taking care of orphans isn't just a "great idea." It's critical. Why? Because every man, woman, boy, and girl— including orphaned and vulnerable children—has been created in God's image and is precious to Him. In Scripture, God describes Himself time and again as the helper of orphans.

Psalm 10:16 praises Yahweh as "King forever and ever." Interestingly, in describing the kingly duties of Yahweh, the psalmist places primary importance on God's care for the weak: "LORD, you know the hopes of the helpless. Surely you will hear their cries and comfort them. You will bring justice to the orphans and the oppressed" (Ps. 10:17–18 NLT).

Other psalms strike a similar tone, extolling Yahweh as "father to the fatherless, defender of widows" (Ps. 68:5 NLT). Jewish scholars point out that God's care for orphans flows directly from His position as king over all the earth.[6] God's people, then, are commanded to care for orphans *as a direct result* of who God is.

As God's messengers, the Old Testament prophets rebuke Israel for ignoring the needs of widows and orphans. God tells His people to stop bringing Him meaningless sacrifices: "When you lift up your hands in prayer I will not look . . . I will not listen" (Isa. 1:15 NLT). Why? Because of the people's failure to care for orphans. "Learn to do good. Seek justice. Help the oppressed. Defend the cause of orphans" (v. 17).

Malachi 3 echoes this same judgment on Israel as Yahweh confronts His people:

> "At that time I will put you on trial. I am
> eager to witness against all sorcerers and adulter-
> ers and liars. I will speak against those who cheat
> employees of their wages, who oppress widows
> and orphans, or who deprive the foreigners living
> among you of justice, for these people do not fear
> me," says the LORD of Heaven's Armies. (Mal. 3:5
> NLT)

In our tendency to place ourselves above Israel, we dare not overlook one of the root causes of God's judgment—failing to care for orphans. When I understood this for the first time, it shocked me. We're not just reading history here. It hits close to home for those of us who haven't considered before that God is commanding *us* to care for orphaned and vulnerable children.

Stop and consider this: Just like the children of Israel, we, as God's people, will be judged for withholding justice from the oppressed and the orphan. If we have the means and the capability to care for orphaned and vulnerable children, yet fail to do so, we are in direct disobedience to God.

There's No Going Back

I am often struck by my past failure to truly care enough to act in the interest of orphans, and it grieves me. For most of my life, I had been so sure I didn't have the time or money for another kid, especially *somebody else's* kid. But when it came to a new car or vacation or even that picket fence, money never stopped us.

It is not as if I—or the church as a whole—was hard-hearted and didn't care about the plight of orphans. I simply did not know the enormity of the problems. No one had seriously engaged the issue of orphan care in any of the churches or schools I attended. But in this case, ignorance is not bliss. Millions of kids around the world are hurting in ways we cannot imagine, and we are called to respond with compassionate care.

Once I was awakened to the issues, God took a formerly anti-adoption guy and began to shape the first National Director of Church Partnerships for Bethany Christian Services, the nation's largest adoption agency. We have more than 1,300 employees, 85 locations in 34 states, and minister to more than 65,000 children and families each year.

God definitely has a sense of humor. I spent much of my life judging Christians who were sidetracked by social justice issues and lost the true gospel message. Now, I spend my time meeting with pastors and educating churches on the needs of orphans around the world. In this journey, I have become increasingly convicted about my lackadaisical attitude—and that of many conservative evangelicals—toward the plight of orphaned and vulnerable children. This is what drives me to write.

Developing a holistic model for orphan care forces us to dive into every aspect of an orphan's struggle, even when it's uncomfortable. The fact is that very few orphans around the world have only to deal with the emotional consequences of losing one or both parents. In addition, nearly all of these children are faced with the nightmare of poverty, human trafficking, HIV/AIDS, deplorable orphanages, abusive foster care situations, racism, and a host of other social evils. In the twenty-first-century American church, we have wrongly dismissed many of these issues, and for that we need to repent. On other fronts we have been silent, and we must now become a voice.

This is not primarily a book about adoption. This book is about *caring for orphans whose lives and plights cannot be separated from complex social issues.* There's a saying within the adoption and orphan care movement: "Adoption is not for everyone, but caring for orphans is for everyone."

Formulating a practical, biblical strategy for global orphan care forces us to confront and wrestle with these challenges that we have not taken as seriously as we should have. If we were honest, many of us would have to admit that we have no clue how to respond, beyond well-meaning prayer or writing a check. We have relegated these social justice issues to the secular world, but if we truly desire to care for orphans, we must be willing to address and respond to their deepest needs.

We can't care about orphans without caring about their daily reality of poverty, HIV/AIDS, trafficking, and other horrors. We can't honestly be satisfied with children living out their entire childhoods in orphanages that our churches have built and then being cast into what is often an even more terrifying reality on the streets when they turn eighteen. As we grapple with the complex situations of orphaned and vulnerable children, we will see that if we reduce the number of orphans in the world by placing them in families, it could dramatically affect the number of HIV/AIDS cases, the number of children trafficked, and the number of children living in poverty.

As an interest in orphan care and adoption ministry begins to sweep through the American church culture, we can't just treat it like a one-week summer VBS. We need "Orphan-focused Sundays," but we also need far more—*we need orphan-focused churches*. Choosing to stand by and do nothing where we see injustice, suffering, and evil is wrong. It is sin. We must take active steps to care for orphans. To do anything less is blatant disobedience.

CHAPTER 2

We Can't Handle the Truth
Orphans and Human Trafficking

J ohnny, what would have happened to your little girl if she hadn't been adopted?" My friend Matt's words cut through the cool night air as we leaned against his pickup truck while watching our sons' baseball practice. Xiaoli came running by, laughing with glee as she dodged behind me to avoid getting tagged, then bolted off across the parking lot.

I ran after my precious girl, scooped her up in my arms, and planted a big kiss on her cheek. My heart flooded with overwhelming love and the strong desire to protect my daughter. I reminded her of the dangers of running in a dark parking lot, especially because she couldn't hear a car engine or horn. She looked up into my eyes with a smirk, and if she could have spoken, I knew she would have said, "Gosh, Dad, I'm a big girl!" She wiggled out of my arms and rejoined the kids on the playground.

As Xiaoli ran to her friends, I was struck by the transformation I saw in her. She was beautiful, headstrong, full of life, happy . . . and free. I didn't want to think about the answer to Matt's question. I didn't want to consider what would have happened to my daughter if she had remained in the orphanage in China.

My mind drifted back to our recent visit to an orphanage in Xiaoli's province. Knowing that we had adopted deaf children, one of the workers introduced us to Xiao Qing, a deaf teenage girl. She could read and write at a very elementary level, but she did not know sign language, so we could not communicate.

Her situation was tragic. Xiao Qing was about to turn eighteen. At that point, she would no longer qualify to live in the orphanage and would be turned out into the streets with no real communication skills, no language, and no family. Her future would likely involve drugs, prostitution, and perhaps even suicide. If Xiao Qing were lucky enough to get a job, she would be paid an extremely unfair wage, and she would likely be abused.

For a moment, all I could see was my daughter standing there. If we, or someone else, had not adopted Xiaoli, her future prospects would have been no different than Xiao Qing's—living on the streets, sleeping wherever she could find a dry spot, unable to communicate, and addicted to drugs. More than likely, Xiaoli would have been trafficked—taken into custody against her own will, her body sold for men's dirty pleasure over and over and over again.

If this were to have been her future, statistics say that Xiaoli would have contracted HIV, which would have eventually stolen her life away, if she hadn't committed suicide first. Alone, a slave, and hopeless . . . would she have seen any other option?

With a heavy heart, I turned back to Matt and finally responded, "You can't handle the truth, man."

The Sobering Reality of Human Trafficking

Human trafficking is an understandably difficult crime sector to gather statistics on, but the International Labour Organization estimated that in 2012 there were 20.9 million people in forced labor worldwide, and 26 percent of those slaves were children.[1] The number is roughly equivalent to the number of Africans in slavery during the seventeenth and eighteenth centuries. Different organizations vary on statistics of the average lifespan of a child once he or she has been trafficked, with estimates ranging from two to seven years. The vast majority of victims are never rescued.

According to the U.S. Department of Health and Human Services, the human trafficking trade is second only to drug dealing as the largest criminal industry in today's world.[2] The trafficking of humans takes on many forms, including child soldiers, domestic servitude, forced child labor, prostitution, and sex tourism. Some victims are simply kidnapped from homes and orphanages, but many others are lured in by promises of a better life—a roof over their heads, plenty of food to eat, and a steady job. Once the victims discover their fate, they are threatened with death if they try to escape. In many countries, traffickers bribe law enforcement officials to turn a blind eye to this atrocity. As such, legal consequences for drug dealing are often more severe than for buying and selling human beings.

Sex trafficking, in particular, has been referred to by the U.S. Department of State as "an engine of the global AIDS epidemic."[3] Up to 80 percent of sex slaves contract HIV/AIDS. Whenever a slave dies or "wears out"—whether from maltreatment, sexually transmitted disease, health complications, starvation, or drug overdose—there are thousands more women and children on the streets who jump at the chance for a "job." And so the vicious cycle of evil continues. UNICEF reports, "The global market of child trafficking is over $12 billion a year with over 1.2 million child victims . . . Children from age 5 to 15 are traded domestically and internationally as a supply for labor and sex."[4]

Unlike drugs or other crime markets, people can be sold over and over again, so there is no cap on the income that one child

slave can bring in. The profits from one trafficked girl alone can
be as much as $250,000.[5] In 2007, slave traders brought in more
profit than Starbucks, Google, and Nike combined. The United
Nations estimates the annual total market value of human trafficking to be more than $32 billion.[6] Human trafficking is a lucra-
tive business and therefore one that will not easily be stopped. But
we must do something.

The Role of Orphans in Trafficking

The 153 million orphaned and vulnerable children worldwide
guarantee a continued market from which human traffickers can
draw. For children living outside of families, no one will ever
know they're missing. There is no moral outcry, no legal search,
and likely no one who even cares.

In many Eastern European countries, overcrowded orphanages are prime locations for traffickers to pick up victims. Often,
orphans are sent on their merry way with only a bus ticket in hand
to make room for smaller children in the orphanage. Other kids
run away from state institutions because of the deplorable conditions. To the homeless teenager who has no family, a phony job
offer sounds like a dream come true. What these kids don't know
is that they are walking into a living hell.

Trafficked children and adolescents become victims of abuse,
rape, torture, starvation, and exploitation of all kinds. According
to a recent government report, "The common denominator of
trafficking scenarios is the use of force, fraud, or coercion to
exploit a person for profit."[7] These kids may be forced to work as
child soldiers, slave laborers, prostitutes, porn stars, or engage in
a host of other inhumane practices.

It gets worse. Often, children are sold into slavery by their own financially desperate parents. This came to life for me during a trip to China. Waiting in line after an overnight train to Beijing, I noticed a commotion across the crowded station. A mob of girls was pushing, shoving, yelling, and desperately trying to get out of the building. "What's that all about?" I asked my friend Yan.

"This one I hate to see." Yan's voice shook. "Their parents put them on the train last night. They made a deal with people in Bejing to have their daughters work for money. The girls had no choice. The money is sent home to their families."

"What kind of work?" I asked.

Yan sighed and dropped his head. "We don't talk about it."

And neither do we, I thought to myself. In many churches, sex is a taboo issue, and the crime of child trafficking has been relegated to the courts and governments. It's a hard issue to even think about, so we don't. But when we ignore abuse, violence, and evil, we grieve God's heart.

Child trafficking is a huge issue among orphaned and vulnerable children, both globally and here in the U.S. It is estimated that 100,000 to 300,000 American kids are victims of sex trafficking annually and that there are 50,000 sexual predators online at any one time searching for victims. In 2009, a three-day operation across 36 cities and 30 FBI divisions around the U.S. led to the recovery of 52 children who were being victimized through prostitution. Nearly 700 people, including 60 pimps, were arrested on local and state charges.[8]

The Ugly Side of Adoption

"My daughter . . . was kidnapped as I was entering my home. A woman appeared in my backyard and grabbed her out of my arms," a Guatemalan woman told news reporters in 2006. "There was nothing I could do."

In 2008, a Midwestern family adopted a little girl from Guatemala. When they brought her home, they never guessed they were possibly assisting human traffickers.

The girl's birth name is Anyelí. Her birth mother claims that she was abducted as an infant and illegally placed for adoption. Anyelí's captors sold her into the adoption system so, unbeknownst to them, the family's adoption fees actually ended up as cash in the traffickers' pockets. This happy family had no clue about their adopted daughter's history. It wasn't included in her case records with the agency. The file just included an apparently fabricated story of the child being abandoned. The judge in the Guatemalan courtroom where the adoption was finalized did not mention that anything was amiss. Anyelí was too young to remember what had happened to her.

In 2011, a Guatemalan judge hearing the case of the birth mother ordered that the American family return their adopted daughter to her birth mother. Nine Guatemalans, including a judge, were charged in the trafficking case.

A country riddled with poverty and corruption, Guatemala is home to many orphaned and vulnerable children. In 2007, nearly 5,000 Guatemalan children were adopted into the U.S. That same year, government officials took forty-six children into custody from one orphanage alone. Some of these children had been trafficked and sold to the orphanage, where at least five female workers were operating under false identities. Far from rescuing street children, they were organizing kidnappings much like Anyelí's.[9]

This is the ugly side of adoption in our broken world. When unchecked and unregulated, adoption can actually be harmful and dangerous to the children we are trying to help. As I write this today, the United States is currently not accepting adoptions from Guatemala, Vietnam, and several other countries due, in part, to suspected trafficking through adoption.

China has also been in the news recently with stories of healthy infants being stolen from families and then sold to state institutions for profit. Allegations have been made against orphanage directors who are buying children and brokers who are kidnapping infants for profit. Local government officials have even been accused of removing children from families who are breaking the "one child" policy and then selling them to an orphanage that will place them for adoption.

Several years ago, Ethiopia rivaled China in its annual adoptions by American families. But in 2011, the Ethiopian government announced that their Ministry of Women's Affairs office would only process five cases per day, in contrast with the previous average of fifty. By taking a proactive stance against a number of adoption-related issues, including trafficking, the Ethiopian government is cracking down on fraudulent activity and ensuring that only truly orphaned children are available for adoption. Since 2011, the Ethiopian government has identified and shut down several corrupt orphanages, prosecuting the fraudulent staff and administrators. This sends a clear message to traffickers and helps protect children from being kidnapped.

Ensuring ethical adoptions is the heart of the matter. In our desire to live out the gospel by welcoming orphaned and vulnerable children into our families, how can we avoid creating a supply-and-demand issue that rewards those with deviant motives and puts children at risk of being kidnapped?

Does trafficking produce orphans . . . or do orphans produce trafficking? The short answer is yes. Either of these scenarios may be true, based on the circumstances. An unregulated "get every kid adopted" approach is likely to encourage child kidnapping and trafficking. In reaction to this, some have advocated that Americans cut off the market for traffickers by banning international adoption.

Finding Families for Children

What if only Ethiopians were allowed to adopt Ethiopians? Or only Chinese allowed to adopt Chinese? At Bethany Christian Services, we always work to keep families together whenever possible through sponsorship, education, and practical resources that combat poverty through self-sustainable income. In-country adoptions do offer many advantages, including protecting children from the disruption of their culture, language, and community. We are actively working in several countries to place children for adoption with families from their own country. However, in many impoverished nations, parents are struggling to meet the basic needs of their biological children in order to keep them out of the local orphanage. In such cases, taking on the responsibility of another child is not feasible.

It is very important that agencies commit to finding *families for children*, not finding *children for families*. This may sound like just a play on words, but these two approaches to adoption are worlds apart. If agencies are just trying to find children for families, especially American families that have a lot of money to spend, this will raise the demand and could foster more trafficking.

However, shutting down international adoption altogether leaves vulnerable children on the streets or aging out of orphanages, which makes them easy prey to traffickers. In Eastern Europe, orphanages are overcrowded because of poverty and parents' inability to care for their children. In many African countries, genocide, war, famine, and disease have produced countless double orphans. They were not stolen or kidnapped from their parents; they buried their parents.

If these double orphans or abandoned children in Eastern Europe, Africa, China, and other parts of the world are not adopted, their chances of ever being part of a family are very, very slim. They will likely grow up in a state institution until they turn sixteen or eighteen years old and then be turned out on the streets to fend for themselves. With little positive influence in their lives, many orphans turn to alcohol and drugs. Once addicted, they will go to any means in order to survive—even selling their bodies. Very few orphans get a real chance at life. Options for survival are few and far between. For many, trafficking and prostitution may seem like the only way to stay alive.

Wisdom is needed in addressing this issue. We as Christ followers will never overcome this evil by disengaging from it. In our sanitized church culture, it is far too easy to condemn anyone we see living in a "sinful lifestyle." But millions of children around the world today are being forced into selling their bodies and then handing the money over to their pimps. These sex slaves can't just decide one day that they're "done." Their owners—or their early death—will decide that for them.

We dare not continue to ignore child trafficking because we feel it is too complex or too corrupt. If we truly care about orphans as Jesus does, we can't just walk away. For the children who need to be adopted, we must navigate the process with wisdom. We must be willing to wrestle through tough and confusing questions. It's not as simple as walking into an orphanage and picking out a child.

It is also very important for us to recognize another critical aspect of this equation: Trafficking of any kind is sinful and deviant. It is behavior that should outrage any person with a conscience. Especially as Christ followers, we should take a stand, speak up, and act to shut down any type of trafficking. Morally, it is detestable. Numerically and statistically, it is also critical to understand that the incidents of trafficking that fuel adoption are extremely few, especially when compared to the number of children who are forced into child slavery, the sex trade, military service, or any other form of servitude.

When There Is No Easy Answer

Once you open your eyes to the horrific reality of child trafficking, you can't go on living like before. My blood boils with righteous anger as I hear the statistics and read the stories, and I shudder to think of my own little girl's future had she not been adopted.

But our anger must drive us to action to "speak up for those who have no voice, for the justice of all who are dispossessed" (Prov. 31:8). This is a key aspect of the gospel we cannot dismiss— "to proclaim liberty to the captives and freedom to the prisoners" (Isa. 61:1). No longer can we stand idly by while coercion, deception, and brute force rob the lives of vulnerable women and children around the world and in our own communities.

Perhaps you're thinking, like I often have, *What can we really do?* The global magnitude of child trafficking is fueled by corrupt governments and impoverished economies. It's overwhelming and easy to wonder if we can really make a difference. There is no easy answer or magic solution, but here are some key ways that you can begin to engage with this issue.

Educate Yourself

Trafficking is in the news on a regular, if not daily, basis. During the two months prior to writing this book, traffickers were arrested in the Philippines for selling women and girls as sex slaves across Asia. Suspects were detained near the U.S.-Mexican border for attempting to smuggle minors into the U.S. A major trafficking operation was uncovered across several regions of India. A group of Nigerian girls were rescued from an unregistered brothel in Ghana. Authorities discovered a large network of female slaves being traded from Paraguay to Mexico to meet local demands for cheap labor. More than six hundred suspects were detained in China, and nearly two hundred children were rescued. Keep in mind that these are just the stories being reported of the traffickers who are getting caught and the children who are being rescued. Most child slaves are never rescued, and their owners are never caught.

So educate yourself by knowing what's happening in the world. Type the phrase "human trafficking" in a web search or in a search box on a news site's home page, and you'll receive countless hits. You can't work to solve a problem unless you truly understand what the current problem is.

Be Wise in Choosing an Adoption Agency

As you or families you know are considering adoption, be accountable for the type of agency you are using. Do your research and ask questions, such as:

- What type of criteria does the agency have for orphans to be considered for adoption?
- Who is the agency working with to ensure that adopted children are not being trafficked?
- Have there been any investigations against the agency?
- Is the agency involved in other types of child welfare work to benefit and protect children who can't be adopted?

In our fallen world, wherever there is the opportunity to help, there is also the possibility of corruption. Adoption has the potential to drastically change an orphan's life forever, but due diligence is needed.

Reach Out to Local At-Risk Children

Nearly 300,000 American children are at risk for trafficking into the sex industry, the majority of them runaways. ABC News reports:

> Many of the children sold into the sex trade come from broken families or the foster care system. Oftentimes . . . they are looking for an escape and for the one thing they say they didn't find at home, love. [One victim] said that once she was part of the sex trade, she didn't feel she had anyone to turn to . . . she didn't want to go back to her family out of shame and fear, and she didn't feel safe outside the vicinity of the hotels she lived in.[10]

In all likelihood, trafficking is happening right now in your community. Consider ways that your congregation can reach out to and build relationships with at-risk children in your church, area schools, and community. Become a foster parent. Mentor at-risk kids. Host an after-school program. Start a basketball league. Seek out and build relationships with kids in your youth program whose parents are incarcerated or absent. Take a preemptive strike at trafficking in your community by ensuring that vulnerable youth have a safe place and a support system to turn to.

Practice Biblical Sexuality

"Rejoice in the wife of your youth," Scripture commands us in Proverbs 5:18. In today's sex-saturated culture, personal pleasure and satisfaction are paramount. But this "however you like it" mindset fuels the demand for the growing commercial sex industry, including street prostitution, strip clubs, massage parlors, brothels, escort services, truck stop hook-ups, and pornography.

Illicit sex services are just a click away. In many ways, the Internet has become a modern-day slave market, "offering the buyer variety, flexible pricing, and individualized service."[11] The easy accessibility and private nature of pornography can seem innocent enough, but aside from hurting their own marriages, what many users don't realize is that they are supporting sexual slavery and human trafficking. I want to challenge you toward purity and accountability. Create a pledge, such as the Defenders' pledge below, and invite the members of your church or small group to sign it:

> Today I make the commitment to becoming a better [person] and my commitment is demonstrated by the following:
>
> - I will not purchase or participate in pornography, prostitution, or any form of the commercial sex industry.
> - I will hold my friends accountable for their actions toward women and children.
> - I will take immediate action to protect those I love from this destructive market.[12]

"Real Men Don't Buy Sex," the Defenders awareness campaign frankly asserts. When one person buys sex, another person is selling it. We need to realize that most of the "sellers" are not doing so willingly. If we want to stop sex trafficking, we must end the demand.

Get Involved with Organizations That Are Making a Difference

The International Justice Mission[13] is a ministry that is on the front lines of the war against human trafficking. IJM partners with government officials and local communities around the world to investigate trafficking crimes, rescue victims of slavery, bring justice to perpetrators, and provide aftercare to survivors so they can start a new life. A collaboration of social workers, lawyers, investigators, and other Christian professionals, IJM holistically addresses the physical, emotional, social, and spiritual needs of victims, restoring dignity, freedom, and hope to vulnerable women and children.

The IJM website alone offers a wealth of information, including a free handbook with ideas about how you and your church can get involved. Here are a few questions that may be helpful to ask:

- Are your home, church, and community safe places for victims of injustice?
- Are there hidden skills and abilities in your family that could be used to reach at-risk youth?
- Is your family giving financially to the work of justice?
- Is your family passionate about a particular part of the world?

Consider Creative Ways to Engage Others

Don't let the fight for justice end with you. Bring others into the battle. Host a dinner party as a way to introduce people to the reality of human trafficking. Spearhead a Christmas initiative at your church. Or simply encourage a friend to join you in supporting one of the many organizations that fight the slavery of humans.

One community in Virginia came together to start an annual "Run for Their Lives" awareness race.[14] Thousands of runners of all ages—college students, kids, parents, seniors—used permanent markers to write the names of sex slaves on their arms before running the course. The marker wears off, but for many runners, their lives will never be the same. The race has now spread to more than fourteen states, raising money and awareness to combat sex slavery worldwide.

Blue Ridge Community Church of Forest, Virginia, developed a direct partnership with a rescue ministry in Central America that works with law enforcement to raid brothels and liberate child sex slaves. The congregation began to pray earnestly for this ministry, support it financially, and take quarterly trips to encourage the national workers and equip the "rescue house," where victims are brought after being rescued.

Regular updates kept the church body informed and engaged, so when the news came in that two young girls, ages five and seven, had been sold by their parents into slavery, the congregation began to plead with the Lord to guide legal authorities in bringing them to safety. For weeks, there was no word on the girls' whereabouts, and law enforcement feared the worst. But after three months of committed prayer together, one of the church's advocates received a direct call with some astounding news. The girls had been found alive and were safely in the care of the rescue house staff.

Within hours of the call, the news went viral among the church community. Far more than just a "missions moment" on Sunday morning or a special offering, this church has engaged at a deep level to bring justice to the oppressed. Acknowledging that they alone can't attack the global problem, they have wisely chosen to focus on one particular country and partner with an organization working there. Their involvement is not driven by guilt, but by a passion for women and girls to live free of the evil and coercion of sexual slavery, and ultimately, to experience the healing work of Jesus.

The Forgotten Children

It's two in the morning, and nightlife is at its peak in the streets of Hollywood. Prostitutes linger on corners, hoping to get hired just to escape the cold for a few hours. Gangs roam the alleyways, armed and ready. Homeless teenagers cluster together in abandoned buildings and bus stations. Some are high on drugs, some are drunk, and all of them are desperate to stay alive.

These are the forgotten children of the night.

A group of inebriated partiers breaks into a fight outside of a club, and Rihanna's "We Found Love" strikes a drastic contrast with the hopelessness of street life. In the dead of night, an outreach team from The Dream Center hits the streets to get to know these teenage boys and girls who are caught in prostitution. "No one is off-limits on the streets . . . We don't accept the fact that the streets belong to.the devil," Matthew Barnett, founder of The Dream Center, writes. "I believe in feeding programs; however, I believe more in building friendships and long-term relationships because they will produce the change. The food opens the door, and the power of God changes the life."[15]

The Dream Center staff often spends time on the streets at night to reach out to prostitutes. One way they do so is by placing a rose in a prostitute's hand. Without one word, it communicates so much. *You are valuable. You are no longer lost, discarded, abandoned. You are loved. You matter. There is hope.* To a girl whose daily reality is forced sex at the hands of strangers—men who use her body, then cast her aside in disgust—the simple act of someone reaching out to her with no ulterior motive can be overwhelming.

These precious girls and boys matter so much to our heavenly Father who came "to seek and save those who are lost" (Luke 19:10 NLT). Our God longs to proclaim liberty to these sex slaves, to set these prisoners free, to heal their broken hearts and their worn-out bodies, to adorn them with true beauty in exchange for chintzy lingerie, to instill hope in their hearts for a different future, and to speak love into their world of harshness and abuse.

The heart of the gospel is rescue and redemption. God the Father sent His Son into the world to rescue us when we were slaves to sin. As Paul said in Romans 6:6–7, "For we know that our old self was crucified with Him in order that sin's dominion over the body may be abolished, so that we may no longer be enslaved to sin, since a person who has died is freed from sin's claims." Our loving, pursuing Father God set aside the glories of heaven for the stench of this broken world. He left the ninety-nine sheep in safety for the one who wandered into harm. And He beckons us to leave the comfort of our cushioned pews to reach out in love to those children who are enslaved.

I'll never forget the first time that I heard Matthew Barnett speak. My gut reaction was: *Why would you give a rose to a girl who chooses to sell her body just to make money? Give her a job, not a rose.* Fortunately, God began to break my heart that day as I listened to the stories of girls and boys who didn't want to be on the streets but were trapped. God forgive me.

The Dream Center is just one example of a group of Christ followers who are passionately engaged in addressing trafficking. Often referred to as the church that never sleeps, The Dream Center grew out of a vision to "reconnect people who have been isolated by poverty, substance abuse, gangs, imprisonment, homelessness, abuse, and neglect to God and to a community of support." It started as a dream the Lord gave Matthew Barnett in 1994 of buying an abandoned hospital in Los Angeles to use as a safe place for street children.

And now, less than twenty years later, there are more than one hundred Dream Centers across the United States.

Your church may not be The Dream Center in LA, but I guarantee you, God wants to use you to bring hope into the living hell of a child slave's reality.

Seek Him. Ask Him. If you can handle the truth, He will not leave you without an answer.

What You Can Do

ANYONE can read one book about trafficking to educate yourself and your church community. This chapter is only an introduction to the issue of trafficking in the world. The International Justice Mission provides simple fact sheets about trafficking that you can easily read to educate yourself and others. As mentioned in the chapter, make sure you and/or your church are educating potential adoptive couples about unscrupulous adoption practices and helping them understand the questions they should be asking adoption agencies or adoption attorneys. For domestic adoption, make sure the agency or attorney is providing post-placement support and ministry to birth mothers.

MANY can research ministries that are working internationally to rescue children from sex trafficking and begin supporting such a ministry. Do your homework and find out how you can offer support, not only financially, but in other tangible ways as well. This will differ from ministry to ministry. You can begin to advocate for this ministry and hopefully get your church involved at a level of support that allows you and others to tangibly work in this ministry.

A FEW can create a ministry in your community that will be actively involved in rescuing children from trafficking. Talk to local law enforcement to determine what is being done in your own community and what the needs are. Gather others together and begin to pray and strategize about how local churches can come together to reach out to trafficked and vulnerable children. Include law enforcement and social workers in the discussion. Look to ministries like Street GRACE[16] in Atlanta for help starting a ministry in your city.

CHAPTER 3

The Unseen Enemy
Orphans and HIV/AIDS

I had never felt so undeserving to stand before a group of people. Honestly, I knew very little of their daily reality, their struggle to put food on the table, and their fight against a deadly pandemic. I didn't even know their language. Shouts of raw, exuberant joy filled the room as these Ethiopian believers worshipped together. Two thousand people were crammed in a school gymnasium that looked to be at least fifty years old. There wasn't much space, but somehow they found room to dance.

Tears ran down their faces as these Christ followers cried out in prayer. I don't know Amharic, but I gathered from my translator that they were begging God to stop the spread of the horrible disease ravaging their families, creating more orphans by the day, and robbing innocent children of their lives. This disease wasn't tuberculosis or malaria. It was Acquired Immune Deficiency Syndrome, more commonly known as HIV/AIDS, which destroys the body's immune system. There is no known cure.

What was I to say to these believers? Many in the congregation had lost a parent, spouse, or child to the pandemic. HIV/AIDS robs them of their life, their future, and their family.

Most of the congregation lived in extreme poverty, yet when the offering plate was passed, I watched each person put something in the bucket. *This is real faith,* I thought to myself. The whole scene created a striking contrast with many American churches where I had spoken.

I have since learned that Ethiopia has been hit hard by the HIV/AIDS virus, which was transmitted to the country primarily through heterosexual contact. The prevalence rate is actually higher for women than for men. And children are the greatest victims. In 2007, more than 92,000 Ethiopian children under the age of fifteen were living with HIV.[1] In 2009, it was estimated that more than 540,000 of Ethiopia's children had lost at least one parent to the virus, and in many cases those orphans are forced to live on the street due to stigma and discrimination.[2]

All around the world, children cry out at night for parents who are gone. They have names, faces, and dreams, but no families. When I began to see AIDS through their eyes, it changed everything. This disease destroys families and robs children of the safety, protection, and love of a home. Every time a parent dies of this treatable disease, another child is orphaned.

The Virus Is the Enemy

UNAIDS reports that there were 2.7 million new HIV infections in 2010. In one year alone, 1.8 million people died of AIDS-related illnesses, and by the end of that year, an estimated 34 million people were living with the HIV virus.[3] Ten percent of those were children.[4] The numbers have likely not changed for the better in the intervening years.

Where have God's people been in the midst of this tragedy? Largely, we have been passive and judgmental to this epidemic.

We have done very little to alleviate the suffering of the infected or consider how this epidemic affects children around the world.

Why are American Christians so slow or cautious to engage with the AIDS crisis? I believe it likely stems from the disease's origins in the U.S. among the gay male population. When HIV/AIDS was first discovered in the United States in the early 1980s, there was a huge amount of uncertainty surrounding the disease. *Where does it come from? How does it spread? If a person sneezes can I catch it? What about mosquitoes—can they spread it from one person to another?*

At first, it was reported as some type of new cancer, then a rare form of pneumonia. Some wondered if it was modern-day leprosy. In the U.S., several new cases of AIDS were being reported every week.[5] People were starting to die. One thing was for sure— the virus was contagious and spreading among homosexual men at an alarming rate.

As a result, the disease was soon dubbed "Gay Related Immune Deficiency" (GRID). In 1982, the Centers for Disease Control released a comprehensive report on the disease, officially referring to it as Acquired Immune Deficiency Syndrome (AIDS), since evidence suggested it was not restricted to the homosexual community. The virus quickly began to spread among drug users who used infected needles and hemophiliacs who received infected blood transfusions. Immigrants and orphans were also at-risk populations.

Although the terminology changed, the virus's early identification with homosexual behavior stuck. Homosexuality was already a hotly debated issue on the political forefront. The Moral Majority, headed by several influential conservatives, publicly decried the moral evils of homosexuality, drugs, and abortion in order to call Christians to a new level of political involvement. This new focus on morality-based politics, coupled with the timely discovery of the virus, set the stage for AIDS to become known as "God's judgment on homosexuals." It served as prime ammunition for the religious right to call Americans to repentance and support of a biblical foundation for society.

While I agree with most of what the Moral Majority stood for, I do not believe that HIV/AIDS is God's judgment specifically on homosexuals. Scripture makes it very clear that all sickness—from the common cold to cholera to cancer—is part of the curse, a consequence of sin. With the fall of man, illness, disease, and death entered our reality (see Gen. 3:19; Rom. 5:12). In a depraved and sinful world, sin always brings consequences. God's Word is clear that "whatever a man sows he will also reap" (Gal. 6:7). From this perspective, every sickness is God's judgment on sinful humanity.

Since we live in a broken, depraved world, evil and sin affect us deeply. We must deal with health crises like heart attacks and cancer, tragedies like 9/11, Hurricane Katrina, the Rwandan Genocide, worldwide poverty, sex slavery, and much more. It is only God's grace and mercy that sustains our lives each day.

John Piper, senior pastor of Bethlehem Baptist Church, wrote the following regarding the role of guilt and grace in confronting the AIDS crisis:

> All sin comes with a price. And many pay the bill who never did the sin. This means that we must speak carefully about the cause of AIDS. If any epidemic ever spread because of disobedience to God's Word, it is AIDS. But millions are infected because of someone else's disobedience, not their own . . . We are all sinners, which means no one does not deserve AIDS. When the Bible says that "the creation was subjected to futility" by God (Romans 8:20), it means that a

sin-permeated creation will be a suffering-permeated creation.[6]

We oversimplify this issue and miss God's heart when we dismiss HIV/AIDS as God's judgment for sin. While it is certainly true that the virus is often perpetuated by a sinful lifestyle, particularly in the United States, we must not forget the millions of innocent victims who are infected through no fault of their own. As we sit around and debate the theological appropriateness of helping HIV/AIDS victims, these men, women, and children live in the daily reality of great physical anguish and suffering. As the disease progresses, their immune systems are severely weakened, making them vulnerable to cancer, pneumonia, and a multitude of other health complications that eventually lead to death.

Many of us need to change our perspective about this horrible disease. "The virus is the enemy," Kay Warren wisely notes, pointing out how often we see HIV/AIDS victims as the enemy.[7] We need to hate the disease and care for those who are infected or vulnerable to it. While the prevalence of this virus in the United States among the homosexual population certainly muddies the waters, we must not allow Satan to use this as a distraction to prevent the body of Christ from responding to this epidemic with compassion and care. In reality, even if HIV/AIDS was spread exclusively through homosexual contact, we would still be called by God to reach out in compassion, offering humanitarian assistance and the hope of the gospel through repentance.

From Judgment to Love

Regrettably, I once viewed HIV/AIDS as the "death penalty" for sexual sin. In my mind, the gay men who contracted the virus deserved it . . . and who was I to stand in the way of God's judgment?

I had never met anyone who had the disease, and I hoped I never would.

However, as God began to move my heart to care for orphaned and vulnerable children, I began to see the many faces of this epidemic. A young boy is raped and forced to serve as a child soldier; a girl is molested by a "trusted friend"; a hemophiliac receives an unscreened blood transfusion; a child is born with the virus; a girl is kidnapped and forced into prostitution. They all, through no fault of their own, contracted the virus that is one of the greatest killers of children worldwide.

These children are sick. They are suffering. They are outcasts.

God really began to convict me of my condemning, condescending attitude toward the HIV virus and its victims. I was shocked to discover that the majority of HIV/AIDS victims are heterosexual men, women, and children living in underdeveloped countries.[8]

It is pretty clear from reading the Gospels that Jesus spent the majority of His earthly ministry reaching out to the sick, the blind, the lame, and the outcasts. Jesus healed the daughter of Jarius and the woman with the issue of blood (Mark 5:21–43). At the Pool of Bethesda, Jesus healed a man who had been a paralytic for thirty-eight years (Mark 2:1–2). When He went to Peter's house, He saw Peter's mother-in-law lying sick with a fever. Jesus reached out and touched her, and the fever left her (Matt. 8:16–18). He healed the man whose body was swollen with fluid (Luke 14:1–6), the man with a withered hand (Matt. 12:9–13), and the man who was deaf (Mark 7:31–37). He healed many people who were ostracized because of an infectious disease called leprosy (Luke 5:12–15).

And not one time did Jesus ask, "So, how did you get sick? What sin did you commit to deserve all this suffering?" If we are going to be like Jesus, we must rethink our tendency to obsess over how HIV/AIDS victims are infected rather than how we can help them. Should that really be the measuring stick for whether or not we minister to a man, woman, or child who is suffering? It wasn't for Jesus. He certainly didn't condone sin, but He spent a lot of time helping sinners.

I can't remember Jesus singling out certain diseases for which He would show no compassion. If HIV/AIDS had existed in first-century Palestine, I'm pretty sure Jesus would have been reaching out to victims of the disease, not shunning and judging them, as I did for so long. "I was sick and you took care of Me," Jesus told His followers. "Whatever you did for one of the least of these brothers of Mine, you did for Me" (Matt. 25:36, 40).

"Jesus has AIDS." That's how Russell Moore, Dean of the School of Theology and Senior Vice-President for Academic Administration at The Southern Baptist Theological Seminary, put it. His provocative words challenge us to reconsider the way we view, treat, and minister to those with HIV/AIDS:

> Some of Jesus' church has AIDS. Some of them are languishing in hospitals right down the street from you. Some of them are orphaned by the disease in Africa. All of them are suffering with an intensity few of us can imagine.
>
> Some of you are angered by the statement I typed above [Jesus has AIDS] because you think somehow it implicates Jesus. After all, AIDS is a shameful disease, one most often spread through sexual promiscuity or illicit drug use.
>
> Yes.
>
> Yes, but those are the very kinds of people Jesus consistently identified himself with as he

walked the hillsides of Galilee and the streets of
Jerusalem, announcing the kingdom of God.[9]

Sound extreme? Radical? Offensive? Many of the responses
to Moore's article criticize him of being liberal and even heretical. Among some religious conservatives, the theological quills
definitely came out (maybe yours are right now). We don't like
to associate sweet, loving Jesus with the shame of a disease often
spread by sexual promiscuity. But Russell Moore's point here is
valuable—we as Christians have largely ostracized those with
HIV/AIDS. We have not loved them as we love ourselves. We have
not seen them through Jesus' eyes. We have been more preoccupied with judging than helping. It is time to change our mindsets
and ask: How can we help and minister to people with HIV/AIDS
like Jesus would?

In ancient Capernaum, a sick man lay paralyzed on his mat
(Mark 2:1–12). He was too weak to move. I imagine he had given
up hope many years before. But the day that Jesus came to town,
everything changed. The paralytic man's friends hoisted his mat
onto their shoulders, fought through the crowds in the busy street,
climbed to the top of a building, dismantled the roof tiles, and
lowered the sick man down right in front of Jesus.

I'm sure there were a few strained muscles and sweaty faces
that day. I personally don't find the idea of fighting through
crowds and scaling a roof with a sick man in tow all that glamor-
ous. But these friends weren't motivated by a desire for fame or
accomplishment. They were motivated by love and were committed to do everything in their power to help their suffering friend
find hope.

Just like that man in Capernaum, there are many among
us who are suffering. A deadly virus attacks their bodies. They
struggle every day to just survive. They have lost hope. And they

desperately need Jesus. They need to know they are not alone in their suffering.

Could it be that God is calling us to set our stereotypes aside and reach out in love? Are we willing to step out of our comfort zones so that they can find hope?

How AIDS Destroys Families

"You can't care for orphans without caring about AIDS, and you can't care about AIDS without caring for orphans."[10] Elizabeth Styffe, Director of Saddleback Church's AIDS Initiative, gets to the heart of the matter. It's true. You can't separate the two. They are intermingled.

Every three minutes, a child dies from AIDS somewhere in the world. Many orphans are particularly affected by this disease. Robbed of their parents, stigmatized by their disease, and left to fend for themselves, they face impossible challenges. And it is estimated that only a paltry 12 percent receive any type of outside support.[11]

Mentally step out of the comfort of your home, the coffee shop you're sitting in, or wherever you happen to be right now as you read. Try to imagine the world through the desperate eyes of an orphan:

- In addition to the trauma of losing a parent, orphans are often subject to discrimination and are less likely to receive healthcare, education, and other needed services.
- In HIV-affected households lacking community support, food consumption can drop by 40 percent, putting children at risk of hunger, malnutrition, and stunting.[12]

Despite our misconceptions about HIV/AIDS, in most African countries, homosexual behavior isn't the culprit for the spread of the epidemic. Sex trafficking and prostitution fuel HIV/AIDS and can often wipe out the adult population of an entire village. Unfaithful husbands infect their wives, who spread the disease to the next generation in the process of childbirth. Many women who have lost their husbands to AIDS then see prostitution as their only means of survival, which only perpetuates the disease. There is also a cultural belief in some areas that sexual relations with a virgin will cure a man of HIV/AIDS, which only further perpetuates the epidemic.

Many babies contract the virus from their mothers, and half of these infants will die before the age of two. Without proper medication, an HIV-positive pregnant woman has a one-in-three chance of infecting her child—either in utero or through breast-feeding. Mother-to-child transmission can be prevented in most cases when drug treatment is available. In fact, when a pregnant woman takes a single dose of an antiretroviral drug before labor and her baby is given a single dose at birth, that baby's chances of infection are cut in half. But medical help costs money, and for many women living in abject poverty, antiretroviral drugs are not accessible. For lack of proper treatment, which costs about $100 to $140 a year, many infants are born into the reality of HIV/AIDS. The ravages of this disease are the only life they will ever know.[13]

Contaminated blood supplies and unsanitary medical facilities often also play a role in spreading the virus. The cultural practice of female genital mutilation, or female circumcision, infects many young girls with HIV/AIDS due to unsanitary instruments, excessive blood loss requiring transfusions, and laceration of tissue. Though outlawed in many countries, female genital mutilation continues at an alarming rate in Africa, Asia, and the Middle East.

It is estimated that more than 100 million girls have been forced to undergo this intrusive procedure, and 3 million are added to that number each year.[14]

These children are innocent, yet they suffer more than you or I could imagine. This tragic reality should disturb us. It should concern us deeply that children are being robbed of their families, their health, and their future through no fault of their own. These are the stories we never hear about.

That day in Ethiopia changed my perspective on HIV/AIDS. My friend Noel had a similar experience when he was standing in a thatch hut in a Kenyan village. As a pastor, his role on the mission trip was mainly to preach revival services, but as he visited hut after hut with the local pastor, he saw the same tragic story unfolding—a mother with ten or twelve children. Typically, only four or five of the children were her own. The others were orphans from the community. Strangely, the vast majority of these women were pregnant. Many of their teenage daughters, who couldn't have been more than fourteen or fifteen, also had swollen bellies. The situation didn't make sense to Noel because many of the community's fathers and husbands had died of AIDS. How were all of these women pregnant?

Then it hit him. The women were pregnant because they desperately needed food. The only way most of these mothers knew how to provide for a dozen hungry mouths was to sell their bodies for sex. After visiting ten different huts, all with the same stories, Noel couldn't take it anymore. Stumbling outside the village, he sat down in the dirt and wept.

"For the first time in my life," he later told me, "I saw the real impact of AIDS. It stole the lives of this village's fathers and husbands. The women were faced with a terrible choice—prostitution or starvation. It tore me up inside. It changed my life."

These women were not seeking out sexual encounters for pleasure or gratification. No, they were desperate mothers who couldn't stand by and watch their children starve. Many had also taken in orphans, adding to the burden of care. And so they sold the only thing they really had—their bodies. They exchanged their health and their lives for a loaf of bread. This vicious cycle spreads HIV/AIDS and produces a whole generation of HIV-positive babies.

HIV-Positive Adoption

Knowing that our God longs to place every orphan in a family, we must consider the possibility of adoption. While our desire should always be to empower families to care for children in their own communities, when HIV/AIDS takes parents' lives, one viable solution may be international adoption.

For many of us, the idea of adopting an HIV-positive child may be unthinkable. However, with proper medication, an HIV-positive child can live a productive, happy, and fulfilling life. But, what about the social stigma, the health risks, and the fear of the future? These are all important questions to address. Beth and I have wrestled with these concerns in our own journey of adoption.

Beth's sweet smile always gives away her scheming. This time, a little Haitian boy had stolen her heart. An adorable five-year-old with curly dark hair, Alain had lost both parents to HIV/AIDS and was waiting for a family. He was a very cute little boy, but in my eyes, there was one big problem. Alain was HIV positive.

To be honest, I wasn't sure what I thought about that. After exploring this possibility, Beth and I decided to pray about it for two weeks. We committed not to discuss Alain with each other during this time; we would only talk to God about him. At the end of the two weeks, we would come back together and talk about what we felt God was leading us to do.

Ten days into our fourteen-day verbal fast, the 2010 earthquake hit Haiti. As Beth and I sat glued to the TV, we found ourselves thinking the same questions, but not daring to ask: *Where is Alain? Is he alive? Is he okay?*

More than 300,000 were dead. Millions of victims were homeless and injured. The country reeled in a state of crisis.[15] Meanwhile, all Haitian adoptions in process were expedited to move orphans into the safety of a family as soon as possible. However, all further adoptions were frozen to prevent accidental placement of a child whose parents were still alive and waiting to be reunited. Since we had not begun the paperwork process to be matched with Alain, it seemed that the answer to our prayers was clearly "no."

A humanitarian agency organized a major airlift to transport the children who were ready to be adopted from Port au Prince to Miami. Most of the children were being adopted by families through Bethany Christian Services, and since I lived nearby, I volunteered to meet their future families at the airport as they waited to be united with their children. It was a wild experience. I was interviewed on several major media outlets and was prepping to be on NBC Nightly News when I got a call. "Johnny, I just want to let you know these kids are all coming from the same orphanage as the little boy you and Beth were praying about. And here's the crazy part. Communication hasn't been very clear, but from what I understand, there's a possibility Alain might actually be on the plane. He was in the process of being matched with another family the day the earthquake hit, and there's a lot of confusion about the status of his paperwork. Honestly, we don't even know if the family will follow through with adopting him if he is on the plane."

My mind reeled as I struggled to make sense of her words. I sat with the adoptive families, trying to allay their fears, all the while attempting to control my own nerves about being live on the evening news. But ultimately, only one thought raced through my mind: *Am I about to become the parent of an HIV-positive child?*

It turned out to be one of the craziest nights of my life. The plane, set to arrive at 8 p.m., finally landed at 4:30 a.m. Processing the kids through immigration took several more hours. When the Haitian orphans finally met their adoptive families, there wasn't a dry eye. The news on TV wasn't just numbers anymore; it was real children. Orphans had been rescued from the jaws of death.

It turned out that Alain was not on the plane. But Beth and I did a lot of soul searching in those two weeks. I think if I had been better educated, I would not have been so crippled by fear. I later learned that children living with HIV can live productive, happy, and fulfilling lives.

We cannot deny the reality that these kids need a family. With this is mind, education is a critical first step. Bethany Christian Services requires families who are considering the possibility of adopting an HIV-positive child to work through a training kit created by the International Department.[16] My prayer is for more agencies and churches to adopt this approach of investigation and learning. Take a minute to consider some critical questions from the kit's FAQ section:

How is HIV/AIDS transmitted?

There are three main ways that HIV/AIDS is transmitted—unprotected sex with a person with the virus; direct contact with infected blood through contaminated needles, syringes, or a blood transfusion; or from an infected mother to her child during pregnancy, childbirth, or nursing.

Research has not found any evidence that HIV/AIDS can be contracted through normal casual contact. Despite what you may have heard, the HIV virus cannot be spread through drinking out of the same cup, sharing a bathroom, sneezing, coughing, hugging, kissing, playing together, or any other type of normal family contact. If you adopt an HIV-positive child, you will need to take precautions about direct contact with your child's blood, such as wearing gloves and using proper disinfectant when you take care of cuts, scrapes, nosebleeds, and other injuries.

What is the difference between HIV and AIDS?

HIV (Human Immunodeficiency Virus) is the virus that causes the disease AIDS (Acquired Immunodeficiency Syndrome). Although HIV causes AIDS, a person can be infected with HIV for many years before AIDS develops.

In some cases, AIDS may not develop. When HIV enters the body, it infects specific cells in the immune system. These cells are called CD4 cells or helper T cells. They are important parts of the immune system and help the body fight infection and disease. When the CD4 cells are not working well, people with HIV are more likely to get sick.

AIDS is diagnosed when an individual's CD4 cell count goes below 200. Even if the CD4 cell count is over 200, AIDS can be diagnosed if the person has HIV and certain diseases called opportunistic infections. These infections, such as pneumonia, multi-drug resistant tuberculosis, toxoplasmosis, and cytomegalovirus, take advantage of the weakened ability of an individual living with HIV to fight off disease.

How long will my child live?

HIV/AIDS is treatable but not yet curable. There is an excellent prognosis for children living with HIV who are able to receive treatment in the United States and other developed countries. With medication and good support, expectations are that children with HIV can plan to live a long, healthy life.

How is HIV treated? Do children have difficulty taking the medications?

HIV is treated through antiretroviral drugs, which greatly increase life expectancy and decrease the risk that HIV will develop into AIDS. However, it is very important that the medications be taken consistently. Many of the medications taste extremely bad. Some children actually require something similar to a G-tube to be placed in their stomachs to receive their medications until they are old enough to be able to take it by pill.

Who should we tell about our child's virus? Should we tell him/her?

This is perhaps the toughest issue for many parents. If you are considering adopting a child living with HIV, you should know the disclosure laws in your state. Federal and state disclosure laws make it illegal to share someone's status without their permission. Of course, your doctor will need to know. Beyond that, it is a personal decision as to who you will tell. Principals, teachers, and school nurses are all people whom you should consider, as they may be at risk should your child need medical care.

No parent wants his or her child to be ostracized or left out. So the question is: At what age do you tell your child? If not, how do you explain the medication? It is critical that adoptive parents consider the budding sexuality of their child as he or she grows older. You will have to disclose your child's status to them at some point, and they will need to understand their sexual limitations.

What about your church? Should you tell them? How would your church react to someone adopting a child that is HIV positive?

Are the nursery, children's ministry, and youth ministry prepared? A pastor friend recently confided in me about this very issue. A couple in his church had been burdened to adopt an HIV-positive orphan. This pastor was quite insistent that the family tell the nursery workers about the child's status. The family was not comfortable with that decision, causing a great deal of tension.

The issue of who to tell is where orphan care, particularly for HIV-positive kids, gets messy. It's a difficult question, but the reality is that there may already be children in your church who are HIV positive. Perhaps a little boy in the pre-K class with a blood disorder contracted the disease through a contaminated transfusion. Or maybe a little girl in the nursery acquired the virus from her drug-addicted mother during childbirth.

Wisdom is definitely needed to take necessary precautions to ensure the health of all the children and workers in ministry programs. Whether you live in a small town or big city, your children's ministry should already be following standard procedures that will protect workers and children from spreading any communicable diseases. Regardless of whether or not you will be adopting a kid with HIV/AIDS, educate your church on standard healthcare procedures. Explain that HIV/AIDS and many other diseases do not know the boundaries of geographic regions or economic status. Your church is not the exception. Every church needs to be a place where all kids are accepted and loved. When fear and stigma leads us to completely oust children with transmittable medical disorders, such as HIV/AIDS, we hurt children.

While adopting an HIV-positive child brings a unique set of challenges, it is also an incredible blessing. I recently received the following note from an adoptive family:

> We have five beautiful children; two of them
> are adopted and are living with HIV. Daily life

for our adopted children is not much different
than for our biological children. Adopting an
HIV-positive child has some minor challenges
that will require education, training, and prayer;
however, the blessing is not only that the lives of
two children have been changed forever, but also,
throughout this journey God has forever changed
the hearts and minds of our entire family. How
is God a father to the HIV-positive orphan? The
answer—through me and you.

Change Starts with You

Far from leading the charge to confront this epidemic, evangelicals have largely ignored the issue of HIV/AIDS. For this, we
must repent. God is calling us to be Jesus to the sick and suffering.

Franklin Graham, president of Samaritan's Purse, calls the
church to action and to lead the way in engaging with this international crisis:

> We as the church have been too quick to
> pass judgment on this disease. Jesus said, "Judge
> not lest ye be judged." We need a new army to
> go around the world to fight this battle, with
> the church of Jesus Christ in the leadership. We
> should be leading, not following or watching this
> fight. Let's stop waiting for the government or the
> medical and scientific industry to solve this prob-
> lem. Let's put this issue at the top of our agendas
> as individuals, churches, denominations, and
> Christian organizations.[17]

As long as we live in a sinful world, sickness will be a reality. Thoughtful, biblical engagement with the reality of HIV/AIDS among orphans may result in a number of responses, including:

- Funding antiretroviral drugs to stop mother-baby transmission
- Training women in micro-enterprise skills to provide an alternative source of income to prostitution
- Equipping local churches to educate youth about the risks of sex outside of marriage and the alternative of abstinence until marriage
- Filling in the gaps to ensure that vulnerable children have access to nutrition, healthcare, and education

Saddleback Church has had a huge influence in this discussion over the past several years. They have developed an entire ministry dedicated to helping those with HIV/AIDS. We must remember that every time we extend the life of a parent with the virus or disease, we prevent another child from becoming orphaned. Not only that, but we can also help improve the lives of children living with the disease by addressing their immediate needs.

The church has a website dedicated to ministering to people with HIV/AIDS and offers the following acrostic—CHURCH—to help us think about practical ways of getting involved:[18]

C – Care for and support those infected and affected. We can personally get involved in the lives of those who are infected or their family that is affected.

H – Handle testing and counseling. We can be an advocate for promoting testing and then counsel people on how to get help if they are positive. This could be done in your own city or in an

international work that your church is already
involved in.

U – Unleash a volunteer labor force. Get
others involved. You can organize others to get
involved through education and small projects.
You don't have to travel all the way around the
world to minister to someone with HIV.

R – Remove the stigma. I heard one story of
a couple who was ministering to some Chinese
people who were HIV positive as a result of
selling their blood plasma. They held a worship
service for these precious people. In a video I saw
one man who would only stand behind a curtain
and peer into the room with one eye because he
was so ashamed. By the end of the night, he was
worshiping with the others and weeping as he
received their love and friendship.

C – Champion healthy behavior. We can use
Scripture not as a heavy stone, but as a soothing
balm to help others understand the importance of
the biblical principles of healthy behavior.

H – Help with nutrition and medication. If
you have a friend who is HIV positive, you could
be their accountability partner in helping them
eat right and take their medications on time. The
schedule of taking pills and getting appropriate
nutrition is critical. If our churches are partnering
with international churches, we must help them
understand the importance of this issue and how
to set up proper accountability partnerships.

As the letters of this acrostic on the previous pages suggest, the local church community is vital in caring for those with HIV/AIDS. We know the power of the local church to change the culture of a city. It's not only about Americans adopting. We must empower our sister churches overseas to care for the HIV/AIDS orphans in their own communities. I saw this firsthand in Ethiopia, where the disease is rampant. Orphaned children are now living in families and some of the local Christian families there are even adopting these children. Let us not underestimate the positive force of the church in taking children off the street and out of orphanages and placing them in families. We may not be able to heal the sick as Jesus did, but we can commit to making sure that no HIV/AIDS orphan dies without a family.

When Obedience Is Risky

Will you dare to take a risk, reach out, and live out the gospel to the victims of HIV/AIDS? I plead with you, for the sake of the millions of AIDS orphans who are suffering right now, to consider the possibility that God might be calling you to do something to help them. One day you will stand before Jesus, and in that moment, He will say, "I was sick and you . . ." You did what? "You cared for Me? You gave Me antiretroviral medication that saved My life? You provided Me with food, clothes, and an education, even though I'd lost My parents to AIDS? You welcomed Me into your own family?" I pray that Jesus can give one of those answers instead of saying, "You did nothing."

Your decisions today will determine what He says to you on that day. Because, yes, Jesus does have AIDS. When we care for the sick and the suffering, we will find Him there.

What You Can Do

ANYONE can begin supporting HIV/AIDS-related work internationally. There are many creative programs designed to specifically help orphans living with HIV/AIDS. There are also programs designed to prevent children from becoming orphaned by providing medicine and proper nutrition to parents living with HIV/AIDS. One excellent example is the Milk and Medicine Program in Zambia.[19]

MANY can volunteer at a local clinic that tests or treats those living with HIV/AIDS. Because of the stigma associated with HIV/ AIDS, becoming friends with those infected will help you not be as nervous around people who are positive. If you know of someone who has adopted a child with HIV/AIDS, you can volunteer to babysit for the child. You can also reach out personally to HIV-infected people in your own community and in global missions efforts to provide support, encouragement, and care.

A FEW can start an HIV/AIDS-related ministry in your church that will educate families and encourage them to consider adopting HIV-positive children as the culture of the church becomes more open and accepting to the HIV-positive community. A FEW can also consider adopting a child living with HIV/AIDS. I have tried to be realistic in this chapter about challenges along the way, but the blessings far outweigh the challenges. More countries are beginning to allow these children to be adopted internationally. For many children, it really is their only hope of survival. Toolkits, such as the one mentioned in the chapter, will help you gain the knowledge you need to make an informed decision.

CHAPTER 4

Home Sweet Home
Orphans and Orphanages

M an made orphanages for children, but God made the family for children." The words slipped out of my mouth as I sat with a group of Ethiopian church leaders, discussing the needs of the country's six million orphans.[1] Silence fell over the small, dimly lit room. I began to evaluate my statement, realizing that my translator, Kelile, was also the head of the local orphanage. Turning to meet his gaze, I was shocked to see tears in Kelile's eyes. We stared at each other for a good thirty seconds without saying a word. Then he put his hand over his heart and said three words that I'll never forget.

"This is right," he said with conviction, brokenness, and honesty.

Kelile turned back to the pastors and translated my words into Amharic, the local language. I then paused to let it sink in. I saw that many of them, just like Kelile, were contemplating the gravity of this statement. To be honest, at the time, I didn't even grasp the full impact of my words. It is a truth that none of us could deny in that moment, at least on a theological level: God made the family for children. He never intended for the growth, nurturing, and development of childhood to happen in an institution.

But what are the implications of this understanding of *family*? It's radical, earth-shattering, and overwhelming because it raises the question of responsibility. Many of the world's orphans live on the streets, struggling just to stay alive. Eighteen thousand children die every day of hunger and malnutrition.[2] Thankfully, some of these children have found safety in orphanages, where they are provided with food, shelter, and education of some kind.

However, as we wrestled through this issue together, my Ethiopian brothers and I were faced head-on with an uncomfortable but undeniable truth: *As followers of Jesus, we cannot be satisfied with children living in orphanages as a long-term solution.*

Traveling with a team from Bethany Christian Services, I was meeting to strategize with these Ethiopian church leaders who live on the front lines of orphan care. To me (and to most of you reading these words), orphan care may seem like a good idea. As we sit on the couch or at the coffee shop, it's easy to hear the stories and *feel* burdened.

But for these pastors, extreme poverty is a reality. Many of the men and women I sat with were fathers and mothers who could barely keep food in their own children's stomachs. Surrounded by needy and starving families, most of these church leaders felt paralyzed to do anything. Yet, as we studied Scripture together, we could not deny that biblically, every follower of Jesus—and the church at large—has a responsibility to take care of orphans.

I was humbled by the passion of these men and women—followers of Jesus who had very little materially, but far more faith than I. As we talked, prayed, and strategized, we realized that these Ethiopian pastors held at their fingertips tremendous potential to turn the tide in orphan care. As an American, I could give money to build an orphanage. But these church leaders had the opportunity to do so much more. They could place orphaned and vulnerable children in homes, not just institutions.

"Orphan ministry is not just an American church thing," I realized as the words came out of my mouth. "And it's not just a command; it's a privilege." Some of the pastors were tracking with me while others looked at me like I was crazy. After all, how could orphans be cared for without orphanages?

The team and I continued to discuss with these Ethiopian leaders a new idea called community-based care. This approach takes children out of orphanages and places them into a temporary foster home or an adoptive home in the same community as the orphanage. Because of the pervasive poverty in their communities, the idea of families taking an unknown orphan into their homes was overwhelming. Though my Ethiopian brothers understood community-based care in theory, they still had questions about the financial burden it would have on their families.

Honestly, as a pastor myself, I was in new territory. My background was not in child welfare or social work, and community-based orphan care was not my idea. A team of professionals at Bethany, headed up by Pamela Harrington and Tendai Masiriri, had developed an increasing discontent with orphanage conditions, and they birthed a vision for orphan care that engaged the church and community. And so we sat among the church leaders of Ethiopia—discussing, wrestling, and strategizing.

A former orphan from the continent of Africa, Tendai led the way in engaging his own culture to understand and begin to incorporate a community-based model of orphan care. I was all ears. I had a lot of questions but few truly satisfying answers. Learning from Tendai and the others, I was amazed at the opportunity that community-based care could bring to children and to the church.

Years later, the words that haphazardly tumbled out of my mouth that day are now rooted in my personal convictions: *Man made orphanages for children, but God made the family for children.* I honestly believe that God never intended for one child to live in an orphanage.

The Reality of Orphanages

Please know that I am not bashing orphanages. I understand that in impoverished countries and under current conditions, some orphanages are necessary. They provide a place of safety and shelter to vulnerable children. The kids get a hot meal and a place to sleep. In some cases, children are even exposed to the gospel and find spiritual nourishment in an orphanage. Though these conditions are less than ideal, orphanages can save the lives of children who would otherwise starve or die of exposure.

This is a good thing. *But is it the best thing?* Anyone who has traveled and visited an orphanage knows the grim reality of this kind of lifestyle. The sponsorship pictures don't show everything. Orphanages are not inherently evil, but let's be honest. A child never enters an orphanage under good circumstances, and an orphanage can never replace the family. I definitely believe that it is better for a child to live in an orphanage than to live on the streets, so I am not suggesting that from a pragmatic standpoint we shut down all orphanages tomorrow.

However, as Christians, we must not simply be satisfied with a child living his or her entire childhood in an orphanage. It just doesn't seem to line up with God's plan for the family. I believe that God grieves for every child who is living in an orphanage because that situation was never meant to be. It may be a temporary "fix" in a time of crisis, but as a long-term solution, orphanages simply aren't enough to nurture children as God intended.

If this statement is true, or even if it *might* be true, then followers of Jesus have a responsibility to pray, research, strategize, and do everything in our power to provide orphans with families. Looking back through Scripture, there is not one mention of an orphanage. God's plan for children from the beginning was the family.

Apparently, society has not always provided orphanages. The earliest mention in recorded history of orphanages being established is not until the early second century. Holding to the belief that every human life was precious, early Christians cared for orphans by taking them in as their own children. Life expectancy at the time was only about thirty years, so many children were left fatherless. In contrast with the Jews, the Romans did not share universal respect for life, so they were fairly disengaged from the orphans in their midst.

The Roman emperor Antonius Pius, however, serves as an exception. Antonius is remembered as a merciful ruler who considered the plight of orphans. During his reign in AD 138–161, he implemented some of the first Christian social services at a government level. These shelters served as an initial place of refuge for orphans. However, the fatherless continued to be raised primarily in the homes of Christ followers up until the legalization of Christianity in AD 313.[3] As Christianity became more accepted and less persecuted, history tells us that Christians sought out new ways to care for orphans:

> The Christians founded hospitals, and children's asylums were established in the East.
> St. Ephraem, St. Basil, and St. John Chrysostom built a great number of hospitals. Those for the sick were known as nosocomia, those for poor

children were known as euphotrophia, and those
for orphans, orphanotrophia.[4]

Literally, orphanotrophia can be broken down to mean
orphans + *trophos* (rearer, nourisher). Orphanages, then, were to
be places of care, protection, and safety. Infants were cared for
in brephotrophia (*brephos* = child), and poor children were cared
for in ptochotrophia (*ptochos* = poor).[5] Over time, these institutions merged to become what we know today as orphanages.
Orphanages were often built on church property or as part of a
larger monastery complex.

Throughout history, Christian charities have built and supported orphanages. By the thirteenth century, one such group,
The Order of the Holy Ghost, supported more than 800 houses
for orphans. As Christianity began to spread through foreign missionary work, orphan care always followed close behind.

In the early 1800s, one young man in Germany came to know
Christ as a university student. When this man passed away in
1898, more than 10,000 orphans were being cared for under his
leadership. We know him as George Muller, a man of incredible
faith who gave his life to caring for orphans.

Ordinary people have done radical and even dangerous things
to care for the fatherless. Amy Carmichael rescued child prostitutes from the temples of India, providing them a safe haven at
Dohnavur Fellowship. Gladys Aylward worked with the forgotten
orphans of China, leading them across treacherous mountains to
escape invading Japanese soldiers. Mother Teresa championed the
plight of orphans, leaving behind a legacy of 610 missions in 123
countries. And the stories go on. There are too many names to
count of ordinary Christ followers who took seriously their role in
caring for orphans, many of them by building orphanages.

Until only recently, Westerners had a vague idea of orphanages as rescue missions in distant lands. In today's world, however, the reality of life as an orphan has become a very personal issue. Television, Internet, and other media forms have put faces to the stories. We have all seen the heartbreaking pictures and footage that tears away at our self-absorbed individualism. Globalization and international travel have even enabled some of us to hold orphans in our arms and to lay the bricks for orphanages ourselves. It's easy to think we know the challenges orphans face, but we still fail to grasp what life is truly like for many orphans around the world.

Life in an Orphanage

John Lahutsky was born prematurely in Russia in 1990. He had cerebral palsy, and his parents abandoned him when he was eighteen months old. John was discovered several days later and taken to the local orphanage—Baby House 10—by the authorities. John describes the next nine years of his life as a nightmare:

> I spent my days either sitting in a chair or laying on a cot . . . I basically had no one to talk to. No one spoke to you. The blinds were closed and the shades were down. There would be 40 children tethered to their cribs and only one person taking care of them . . . I didn't know what the sun was. I didn't know what a tree was. All day long I was just sitting in a closed room.[6]

John was placed in an insane asylum at age six. Basically, he was left to die. As a handicapped child, he was considered a shame to his family and community. John was raised in this state-run institution that provided him the basics of food and a bed. But he was starved of touch, tied to his bed, neglected, and treated like a number.

Life as an orphan is hard, and some of our favorite stories would argue that, sometimes, these children live miserable lives. Think about Oliver Twist, Anne of Green Gables, Aladdin, or Annie. Many of these stories carry the image of an orphanage as a dark, drab, foreboding place—a place without hope. Remember the pictures of the tall, dull gray building overgrown with weeds that the orphan desperately wants to escape from, with the uniforms, the rows of steel bed frames, the broken windows, and cruel children? Granted, orphanages are not prisons, but even the best ones aren't exactly home sweet home either.

Earlier, I made a radical statement: *I honestly believe that God never intended for one child to live in an orphanage.* Perhaps, like me, you had a negative reaction to that thought. You may have financially supported an orphanage somewhere in the world or even helped build one. Perhaps you have fond memories of holding an orphan at one of those orphanages. But as we investigate what orphans need, I want to challenge you to be willing to consider the idea that while you might have good feelings associated with orphanages, living in an orphanage might not be the best option for children. After all, if we don't allow orphanages to exist in the United States, why are we content to build and sustain them in other countries? The goal of orphan care is caring for orphans, not the good feelings we get from our generosity in building or supporting an orphanage. Orphan care is not about us; it's about them.

God created us to be fundamentally relational beings. We long for community. When a child grows up in an orphanage of fifty or a hundred kids, he or she is robbed of the deep human need to be cared for and nurtured by a stable, loving parental figure. No matter how hard orphanage staff members try, it is impossible to create that "safe haven" relationship with more than a handful of children.

Because of the high child-to-caregiver ratio and changing shifts of caregivers, institutional care inhibits healthy emotional attachments, which are integrally connected with social and emotional development. Children in orphanages lack "stable caregivers and open opportunities for exploration and mastery of the world."[7] A 2010 study of Ukrainian orphanages points out the "negative impact of institutional living on child development and functioning in adult life," particularly leading to mental health disorders.[8] A similar study in Malawi cites orphanages as leading to broken relationships between children's families and communities of origin.[9] Research on Russian orphans reveals the flaws of public upbringing: "A low level of intimacy and trustfulness, emotional flatness . . . [and] disruption of attachment."[10]

Without the nurturing environment of a loving family, institutionalized children suffer significant setbacks emotionally, socially, cognitively, and physically. IQ levels have been found to be significantly lower among these children.[11] A study among Romanian orphanages found that many children suffered from profound learning disabilities or had complex medical needs. Turkish orphans living in institutionalized settings reported significant levels of alcohol and tobacco use, chronic disease, and poor social skills.[12] A review of child behavior in Central American orphanages found "a lack of warm, sensitive, responsive . . . and available caregivers," and common occurrences of mental disabilities.[13]

From Ukraine to Malawi to Russia to Romania to Turkey to Central America, the findings are similar: *Institutional care is, at best, a poor model for long-term orphan care, and at worst, quite harmful to children's development.* As early as 1951, research by the World Health Organization showed "the necessity of giving up orphanages as a model of children's upbringing."[14] A 2011 Turkish study concludes, "[T]his kind of care model—institutional care— has significantly negative effects on the development of children."[15] Delayed physical, mental, and emotional development; reactive attachment disorder; inability to build healthy relationships; an increased tendency toward drug and alcohol addictions; and psychological difficulties are just a few of the negative side effects of institutionalized care.[16]

Is There Any Other Option?

Grappling with the negative realities of orphanage life has propelled me on a desperate search for answers. *Is there any other option that would better provide orphans with a safe, stable, loving relationship?*

A continuum of community-based care offers a hopeful solution to this plight, connecting the community, the church, the orphanage, and the government in an alliance to provide the best possible care for orphans. Over the past several years, I have had the privilege of working with Bethany Christian Services and social workers, government officials, and Christian leaders around the world to implement this revolutionary approach to orphan care. The word *continuum* is critical. There is no one-size-fits-all formula. Every culture, every community, and every child is unique.

Within the strategy of this model, we approach orphan care asking what is best for each individual child, not imposing a Western idea of how it "should be done." This community-based continuum aims to provide care for each orphan and vulnerable child at his or her identified point of need, with the goal of having every child living within a family.

The continuum of care is a complex social work approach to orphan care that includes temporary care, family support, training, adoption, and community education. In layman's terms, we can understand this model in a few simple steps. Basically, we need to answer three questions:

Is there a way to keep the child with his or her family of origin?

The ultimate goal is family support, not removing the child from the family. Often, sponsorships can put money in parents' hands, clothes on their children's backs, and food in their stomachs. Organizations like World Vision, Compassion, and Bethany Christian Services help connect families in the U.S. with impoverished families in other countries who cannot provide for their children's basic necessities. Rather than leaving their children at an orphanage so they don't starve, these parents experience the blessing of the body of Christ coming together in order to keep the family together.

How can we best care for the child temporarily displaced from his or her family of origin?

Currently, orphanages definitely play a role in providing temporary care. However, an orphanage is the starting point for a child, not the dead end. Family illness, emergency, or poverty may lead parents to bring their children to the local orphanage as an act of mercy. In some cases, the orphanage stay is temporary, and the child goes back home as soon as the situation is remedied.

Ideally, orphanages serve as temporary "safe houses" until a child can be placed in community-based foster care or adopted into a family, either locally or internationally. The continuum of care connects the orphanage and associated government office with in-country families (often through the local church) to create a home-based foster care system. This approach opens the door for many, many children who are not legally adoptable to have the opportunity to be raised and nurtured in the context of a family, not an institution.

In an international adoption process, where an agency works directly with an orphanage, the orphanage generally oversees the records, paperwork, and processing, in partnership with a locally-based adoption organization. Similarly, community-based care connects a locally-based organization and the local church with orphanages that can oversee the interview process, placement, and monitoring of children living in foster homes.

Ideally, the orphanage takes on a supervisory and regulatory role, while families from churches in that culture facilitate the actual care of vulnerable children. The agency's local office in the country works alongside the orphanage and the local church to offer culturally appropriate training, support, and supervision to ensure that children are being placed in healthy, nurturing homes.

Eventually, the role of the orphanage as a long-term residence for children can be eliminated. This should ultimately be our goal. How my heart longs for the day when churches celebrate one more orphanage being closed because all of its children are placed in families, rather than reporting on one more orphanage being built on a short-term mission trip.

I know I am making this sound really simple, but it's not. Some children have severe emotional and physical handicaps. Finding families who can provide for these children can be very challenging. There is also the issue of countries that are so impoverished that the number of children in need is far greater than the number of families who are able to provide a nurturing home. Even so, a home for every child should still be our goal.

Working through local churches around the world (which often support and partner with nearby orphanages), we can build a community-based model that is more cost efficient, better for children, and empowering to the local church. Where there are no churches, our mission efforts must focus on planting and helping sustain churches. This is an important way of tying in the overall mission of the church in order to fulfill the Great Commission. Where there are no churches, the gospel needs to be shared with unreached people groups, and churches planted as people come to Christ. As a church is cultivated and grows, believers have the opportunity to care for and open their homes to local orphaned and vulnerable children. This is not quick and easy, but in looking for long-term, self-sustainable solutions, we need to consider church planting as one of them.

How can we provide a permanent, stable, nurturing environment when the child cannot go back to his or her family?

For whatever reason, it may be impossible for some children to return to their families. Their parents may have abandoned them, been killed in a war or natural disaster, or the government may have removed parental rights due to abuse, neglect, or inability to provide care. In these situations, the orphanage serves as a link to adoption—both domestically and internationally. It is through the orphanage that records are kept and the file for the child's adoption is made ready. The orphanage is responsible for preparing the paperwork and making sure no illegal activity takes place in the adoption process.

When legal and feasible, adoption provides children an opportunity to experience family as God intended. Otherwise, orphans—like John Lahutsky and my own adopted children—face a bleak future of being stuck in an institutionalized setting until they are eighteen and then being turned out on the streets.

In addition to adopting children ourselves, we as the American church have the responsibility and privilege of partnering with churches in places like Russia and Ethiopia and Romania so that believers there can adopt orphans from their own communities. This may include offering financial support, prayer, education on adoption, and encouragement to our "sister churches." Some churches in the United States have adoption funds for their members. These same churches should also consider an adoption fund for the members of their sister church on the other side of the world.

In many cultures, adopting outside your ethnic group, tribe, or bloodline is unheard of. As relationships are built between churches in America and churches in these cultures, opportunities arise to train pastors in the theology of adoption, pointing them back to Scripture, not a particular Western model.

As I write this, a group of adoptive parents partnering with Bethany is traveling to Ethiopia to meet and spend time with local believers. They will sit down and talk about the blessing and biblical basis for adoption and share their stories to encourage these Ethiopians to consider adopting Ethiopian orphans.

By engaging pastors, individuals, and communities, the adoption culture can begin to spread. How I long for the day when I won't just hear about the family at my church who traveled around the world to adopt an orphan, but also the family on the other side of the world who chose to adopt an orphan from their own community and was able to do so because of the financial and prayer support of their sister church—my church.

This approach to caring for orphaned and vulnerable children places the priority on the best interest of the child. Implementing this model at Bethany, we have found it to be biblically sound and revolutionary on multiple levels.

I would dare to argue that a continuum of community-based care offers the best for every party involved. Here's why:

- Children are removed from the orphanage and placed into Christian homes.

- American churches are able to fully engage in mission efforts through partnership with a local church in that country.
- A local office, such as Bethany Christian Services, insures the accountability aspects of this program.
- Professional social workers oversee the program to make sure the best decisions are made on behalf of the children.
- As U.S. churches complete mission trips with partnering churches abroad, the U.S. sponsors are able to see their investment firsthand, creating a personal connection.

Due to the success of community-based care in Ethiopia, Ghana's government has asked Bethany Christian Services to bring the program to Ghana. The national leadership shares the conviction that children should ultimately be placed in families, not orphanages.

Catching the Vision

Rwanda is another powerful example of community-based care. After the countrywide genocide in 1994, more than a hundred new orphanages were started. As of 2012, seventy of those orphanages have been closed, and the children have been placed back with their families, with adoptive families, or in foster care. Though one of the poorest countries in the world (60 percent of people live below the poverty line),[17] Rwanda is changing the future of their children by placing them in loving families.

Rwanda's Prime Minister Habumuremyi said, "There is need to bring up these children in a family environment because these children need parental love and care to grow well. I am very sure if we all make the decision to adopt these children, the issue of orphans can be done away with. Children raised up in families are assured of security from all kinds of abuse and also assured of growing up with family values."[18]

Just to be clear, the prime minister's emphasis is on Rwandan families adopting Rwandan children. Domestic adoption is always less expensive for all involved and less traumatic for children, since they can continue to live in their own culture.

Adoption and orphan care should not just be an issue for the American church, but also for the global church. Churches in Sudan should be encouraging their members to adopt Sudanese children; churches in China should be encouraging their members to adopt Chinese children; and so on.

Sadly, money is usually the issue that makes in-country adoption impossible in developing countries. And money is the very resource that many Americans have to offer. In addition to using that money to sponsor children, churches in the U.S. can send mission teams to specifically visit and support their sister church overseas. These mission teams can include adoptive families from the U.S. who can share their stories, struggles, pains, joys, and victories experienced in adoption. This type of interaction will help Christ followers from a culture where adoption is a strange idea begin to understand it as a biblical command and even a joy and privilege.

A continuum of community-based care not only places the fatherless in families, but also offers churches in America the opportunity to get involved at a grassroots level with orphan care through partnering with a specific community in another part of the world. By supporting the work of local churches around the world in caring for orphans, American believers can do far more than we could ever accomplish on our own. After all, our brothers and sisters in that country live among their orphans. They know the culture, the language, and the unique struggles. As we partner with them—financially, in prayer, and by our presence—we hold up their arms in ministry, empowering their outreach and creating a beautiful image of the worldwide unity of believers as the hands and feet of Christ.

During my time in Ethiopia, we visited a local orphanage, and one little boy latched onto me the entire time. As we left, one of the workers had to literally pry him out of my arms. On our long drive back to the hotel in the city of Addis Ababa, I sat in the back of the van, listening to my iPod and trying to go to sleep. I couldn't.

A song came on that I didn't even know was on my iPod: "Best Day" by Taylor Swift. The song tells the story of how Taylor's family has always been there for her. Whether the days are good or bad, as long as she has her family, every day will turn out to be the "best day." She reminisces about spending a day at the fair and then falling asleep in her mother's lap on the way home. She sings about the day the kids at school made fun of her, but when she got home, her mom took her shopping until she forgot about those bullies. Many nights back at home, my daughter Heather would sing this to me and Beth while I played it on my guitar.

As I listened to the words that night, all I could think about was that little Ethiopian boy I had held in my arms just a few minutes earlier. *Who will be there for him when he makes an A on his report card? Who will be there for him when he misses the winning goal in soccer and tell him that it really is okay and that he can try again? Who will be there for him when he finally makes the winning goal and needs someone to give him a bear hug and say, "That's MY son!"? Who will be there when his classmates make fun of him for being an orphan?*

I thought about James and his basketball games through our church's league. The first year, he was easily the most uncoordinated kid on the court, and by the end of the season, even the opposing team cheered for James to score his first basket. Every time he had the opportunity to shoot, the entire gym grew silent with anticipation as the ball flew toward the net. But it was the same result every week—he missed.

It was obvious that James had a few more challenges with his bones and muscles than the other kids, but his smile and incredibly positive attitude won the crowd over. However, on the drive home every week, James stared out the window blankly, trying to hold back the tears. He really wanted to score. And every week I had the privilege as his dad of putting my arms around his skinny little body and reassuring him, "James, I am so proud of you, and I love you just the way you are. I can't wait for you to score a basket, but I love you now."

That night in Ethiopia on the road back to Addis Ababa, I'm so glad it was pitch black in the backseat of the van. I cried uncontrollably for at least thirty minutes, because I knew the tragic answer for that little boy at the orphanage.

Who will be there for him? *Nobody.*

That's when it hit me like never before—man made orphanages for children, but God made the family for children.

What You Can Do

ANYONE can consider and evaluate the orphanages and/ or children you are supporting. Talk to the organization you are working with to discuss their long-term goals for these children. If your sponsored child is living in an orphanage, ask if the goal is to place him or her in a family. If not, ask why not. If it is, ask for stories of children whom they have removed from orphanages and placed in families. Talk with the missions pastor or missions team at your church about the long-term goal of orphanages they are currently working with or supporting. Change won't happen overnight, but you can at least start a discussion about community-based care and the biblical model of placing kids in families. Remember that there are many social and cultural issues involved, and this may not be a quick or easy transition.

MANY can start an adoption fund in your church that helps pay for adoption expenses of those in your partnering international churches. If you partner with a church or group of churches from another country for community-based care, you will want to encourage domestic adoption. In many countries, domestic adoption is a simple and inexpensive process compared to the United States. However, the expenses are still great for those who live at the poverty level. You and your church can ease this financial burden by providing the finances for families willing to adopt in their own countries.

A FEW can be part of or support a mission team that travels to and meets with pastors and families in other cultures to talk about the biblical meaning of adoption and what it is like to be an adoptive parent. Expose them to community-based care and reach out to government agencies that are open to this concept. The team should include adoptive parents as well as a pastor. The pastor can train area pastors on the theological understanding of adoption and the role of the church, while the adoptive parents can host question-and-answer times with prospective adoptive families.

CHAPTER 5

The Problem with Bootstraps

Orphans and Poverty

There was no night-light to ward off the "monsters," no cozy pajamas, no stuffed animals, no warm milk to fill a hungry belly, no comforter to snuggle up under, not even a pillow to lay a sleepy head on. As I looked at the plywood scrap that James slept on at the deaf school, I fought back tears. I imagined our son sleeping on this makeshift bed every night with his friend Wang Bing Bing. A thin blanket and shared body heat was all that kept the boys warm in the extremely cold Chinese winters.

Standing in the primitive four-room dormitory of James's deaf school, I was shocked by the horrifying conditions these fifty kids woke up to every day. The tiny room was lined with triple-decker beds made from old metal frames and plywood. Mold and mildew covered the walls of the dimly lit room.

The headmistress took us out to show off their prized possession. I was expecting a swing set, a jungle gym, or maybe even a puppy. I certainly was not expecting a huge trash pile. This garbage was their lifeline; it provided fuel for cooking and for heat. The school staff used the trash to stoke a small potbellied stove—the only heat source in their dormitory.

Next to the trash pile was a concrete structure that looked like a fifty-five-gallon drum rigged as a stove. There was a hole in one side to stoke the trash fire, and a rice pot sat over a small opening on top. The school staff cooked for fifty hungry kids in this open-air "kitchen" year round, through rain, sleet, snow, and heat.

Burning trash to cook rice. It's a stark contrast with our family's regular crockpot dinners, where cooking is as simple as plugging the cord into an electrical outlet that delivers unlimited energy to our home.

As an orphan, James was fortunate enough to have this deaf school nearby. Yes, I said fortunate. In his culture, most special needs kids don't ever have a chance to go to school. The major-ity of James's classmates boarded at the school for twenty-eight days out of the month, and despite the terrible conditions, they considered it a privilege to be able to learn. These kids' parents are some of the bravest people in the world—they fought to take care of their deaf children and provide them an education. They didn't abandon or kill their kids just because they were disabled.

Because of a heavy Feng Shui influence in China, a child with special needs is often viewed as bad luck; he is a curse on his family and community. China's strict one-child policy also complicates the situation. If your one child has a disability, your livelihood and future are at risk, especially if you are destitute. Almost all of James's classmates were from very poor families. In fact, most of the parents couldn't even pay for their kids to attend the deaf school. But Hong, the head schoolmistress, never turned a child away. She knew the power of education in breaking the cycle of poverty. Many weeks, her staff would not even receive their salaries, yet they continued to care for these kids, teach them, and give them hope.

I am so grateful that James had this opportunity. Hong became like a mother to him. She begged the orphanage to let him come to the school. She looked out for him. She held him when he cried. She advocated for him to be placed for adoption. Much of who James is today I owe to this dear woman. Beth and Hong connected instantly because of their shared love for teaching the deaf. Today, we consider Hong as part of our family and stay in touch through regular visits and e-mails. She has become a follower of Jesus and has led more than twenty people to the Lord. Hong continues to pour her heart and soul into her students at the deaf school, serving out of her own poverty.

So what about the other kids? James is part of our family now, but what about his friend Wang Bing Bing and the other forty-eight students? Did they choose this life of poverty? Are they being judged for their parents' sin? Are they lazy? Do they just need to "try harder" and pull themselves up by their own bootstraps?

American children who have special needs or who live in poverty face significant challenges, but James's friends in China fight every day just to stay alive. They fall asleep many nights aching with hunger. Some have bloated stomachs, skin rashes, and other medical issues as a result of a parasite transmitted when human feces are used as fertilizer.

I'll be honest; I still struggle to comprehend this depth of poverty. These days, James grabs his coat, pulls on his boots, and heads out the door to school every morning without a second thought. Most of his friends back in China don't even have boots, much less bootstraps.

The Desperation of Poverty

Are we responsible for these children? I've wrestled with this question many late nights since returning from China. For years

I had heard statistics and seen ads on TV, but never did I dream that my own son was among those numbers.

Today it is estimated that one in seven people in the world are undernourished, and children are the most vulnerable age group. Nearly 5 million children die each year due to poor nutrition and starvation.[1]

If we're really honest, most of us have never experienced true hunger. When we feel the pangs of an empty stomach, we know it's time for lunch. But for many kids in the world, there is no lunch and no dinner. There is no guarantee that they will have any food to eat today, or all week, for that matter. If they do eat, like James's friends, they will likely be consuming polluted food or an unbalanced diet, leaving them susceptible to malnutrition and disease.

Poverty is a complex issue and can be perpetuated by faulty economic systems, war, famine, and disease. There is no quick fix. Shipping pallets of food to feed starving children may provide temporary relief, but self-sustainable solutions that break the cycle of generational poverty are difficult to achieve.

At some point, we must consider a very important and controversial question: When is poverty a valid reason for a parent to place a child for adoption? In a perfect world, no parent should ever be driven to the point of desperation to abandon their child. But in a fallen world with failed systems, corrupt governments, selfish leaders, famines, and disease, abandonment or placing a child for adoption because of extreme poverty are sometimes realities. Critics of adoption are quick to point out that the money spent on an international adoption of a child who has a living parent could be given to the biological family to help them raise the child and provide for food, clothing, shelter, school supplies, and other necessities. Theoretically, I agree.

Unfortunately, poverty cannot be reduced to a mathematical equation. Poverty is a culture.

Our friend Hong at the deaf school wrestled with this very dilemma. A student's family wanted to abandon their son in the hopes that an American family would adopt him and offer him a "better" life. I couldn't scream "No!" loudly enough into the phone as we spoke with Hong about this situation. These parents loved their son so much that they truly wanted what they thought was best, even if it meant never seeing him again. At the same time, they had no idea how abandoning their son would impact him both psychologically and emotionally. It is one thing for a child to lose parents to death; it is quite another thing for a child to be abandoned by living parents.

Very few of us in the U.S. have ever been faced with such a gut-wrenching decision. In our culture, a woman faced with an unplanned pregnancy often meets with counselors to determine what is best for her and her child. Often, these women make a very brave decision to place their baby for adoption instead of try-ing to raise a child as a single mom with little financial resources. It is very difficult for an expectant mother to place her child for adoption, even when she has the opportunity to review a detailed file on prospective parents, perhaps meet them, and then choose them as the adoptive parents of her baby.

However, in China there is no process for adoption. There are no counselors to meet with, no agencies to create a custom adoption plan, and, frankly, there are no legal options to consider. Abandonment, with the risk of being caught and punished, is the only option. When people are living in a culture of poverty, they quickly lose hope. They become desperate, and desperate people resort to desperate measures. Many impoverished parents do not see any possible way to provide for the needs of a child, especially one with a disability. For many, the choice to abandon their child in the hopes of a foreign adoption is believed to be the highest act of love. These parents choose to set aside their own desires and dreams to see their child grow up, and instead, they hope for a different life for their child and a ticket out of poverty.

Before labeling these parents as heartless and evil, we must be willing to crawl inside their reality. Consider the emotional torment of watching your child waste away before your eyes, while you are completely helpless to provide the food her little body needs. Poverty can lead people to do extreme things.

In Our Own Backyard

Poverty and hunger are not just problems in other countries. More than 20 percent of children in the U.S. live below the poverty level.[2] This rate has increased from 17.6 percent in 2006 and is two to three times higher than the rate in most other major Western industrialized nations.[3] Though the guidelines for determining the poverty level are much different in the U.S. than in developing nations, poverty is still a major issue here at home.

I'll never forget the day I met Duante, a kid who lived one county away from our church in Alabama. My friend Turk Holt invited me to come along to visit Duante because he'd been in the hospital again. The doctors couldn't figure out why, but Duante's legs kept giving out. Some days he struggled just to make it to the bus stop. Some days he didn't even make it that far, so he missed school.

As Turk pulled up in front of an abandoned trailer, I asked him, "What are we doing? I thought we were going to visit Duante."

"We're here," he replied as he jumped out of the truck.

I stood there in shock, looking at what used to be a mobile home. Surely, no one could actually still live in this dilapidated structure, propped up unevenly on cinderblocks. But for Duante, this was home sweet home. He lived in this tiny two-bedroom trailer with his mother, grandfather, and four siblings, as well as an over-populated colony of roaches. As we stepped through the doorway, I fought the urge to gag. The smell of mildew, old trash, and body odor was overwhelming. In the dim light, I noticed a thirteen-inch black and white TV playing in the corner. At least five roaches were crawling across the tiny screen.

Duante's mom offered me a seat on an old kitchen chair. I was afraid to sit down for fear of sitting on one of the bugs, so I leaned up against the wall instead. Bad idea. A tickling sensation making its way up my arm quickly reminded me that roaches can climb walls too.

This was my first real experience with poverty in the United States. *No wonder Duante is sick all the time*, I thought to myself. Duante's malnourished body simply couldn't function well, causing temporary paralysis in his legs.

Turk had told me that Duante's oldest brother, Leroy, had been experiencing strange problems at school. Every Monday morning, just before noon, he would get sick and start vomiting. After awhile, the school counselor began to suspect that Leroy was using drugs or alcohol on the weekends and coming to school on Mondays hung over. My friend Turk, who had become like a father to these kids, investigated the situation. What he found broke his heart.

Far from an addict, Leroy was starving. As the oldest child, this courageous youngster felt it was his responsibility to make sure his mother, grandfather, and siblings had food to eat.

Through a school lunch program, Leroy was eating at school, but that was it. He ate one meal a day, five meals a week. Leroy's last meal of the week was Friday at noon. His next meal was lunch on Monday. By 10:30 every Monday morning, Leroy would begin to smell the aroma of food wafting in from the school kitchen. His starving body produced a strong physiological reaction to the smell of cooking food. And so, every Monday, Leroy ran to the bathroom and vomited. Every Monday, the kids laughed at him. And every Monday, his teacher thought he was coming off of a hangover.

Duante and Leroy lived less than thirty miles from my house, but their abject poverty was worlds apart from my plush sofa. More than just hunger pangs, these kids struggled with significant physical challenges because of a lack of food. This wasn't happening in Ethiopia, China, or Haiti; it was in my own backyard.

In the shadow of my church's steeple, Duante lay curled up on a roach-infested couch. He was fourteen years old, but his little body looked more like that of a nine-year-old. I still remember Turk leaning over to Duante's mother and assuring her that he would bring some food over so they could eat. Turk had a gentle tone of voice and overwhelming love and compassion in his face. He did not rob this woman of her dignity or chide her for "neglecting her children."

He knew this family well enough to know that Duante's mother was not irresponsible or lazy. She was willing to work, but her kids still didn't have enough to eat. Were they missing out on government programs? I don't know. Was there more help available? Maybe, but what would our attitude likely be if we were behind Duante's mom in the grocery line and she pulled out WIC vouchers? Would we make a snide remark about the lazy bums who take our hard-earned money? Would we drive off without even bothering to glance at the woman shivering in the cold as she waited to catch a bus? Would we assume she was content to live off of welfare for the rest of her life?

WIC and Waitressing

Not long after Beth and I welcomed a boy from the foster system into our home, I found myself sitting at the Health Department waiting to receive his WIC vouchers. I wished I had a sign to carry that read, "I'm not poor or lazy or anything else you might think," in case anyone misjudged me. I had never imagined that my family would be using government aid. But as part of the foster care arrangements, the state provided his formula and I had to make quarterly trips to the regional office to insure he continued to receive his services. Let me tell you, it was eye opening to be on the other side of the story.

Uncomfortable plastic chairs lined the cramped waiting room, and as I sat waiting for my turn, I watched the folks around me. I wondered about their stories. Across the room, a Hispanic girl in her early twenties picked up her phone and started yelling into the receiver. By her tone of voice, I was glad I didn't understand Spanish. To my right, an older man cracked a toothless grin. To my left, a woman dressed in a waitressing uniform tried to keep three rowdy kids from climbing the walls. My kids were about the same age as hers, so I struck up a conversation with her and found out her name was Carrie.

Carrie the waitress definitely looked frazzled, but she was not lazy. From the dark circles under her eyes, I guessed she had worked the early morning shift through lunch and then picked up her kids from school. She didn't want to be in that government office. She wanted to be at home with her feet propped up.

As I sat there, I thought about my college days of stocking groceries at Winn Dixie. I would go to work at 4 a.m. and work until noon, grab a quick bite to eat, and then go to class until 5 p.m. Many days, I was so physically tired that I would fall asleep trying to study or shut off the alarm clock in the morning without even realizing it. One morning I actually sprayed WD-40 under my arms thinking it was a can of deodorant. Another time, I stopped to get gas, put ten dollars worth in the tank, and went to work. An hour later, a policeman showed up to arrest me for stealing the gas I had forgotten to pay for.

I only kept the job for two semesters. The schedule was grueling, even for an energetic twenty-year-old. But for Carrie, it was her daily reality and her future for the next ten or fifteen years. When you go out to dinner next week and Carrie is your server, remember that she probably has hungry mouths to feed at home. Rather than assuming her bloodshot eyes are from late-night partying, stop and consider that waitressing may be just one of her several jobs. After a twelve- or sixteen-hour workday, she drags her exhausted body home to try and be a mom.

As Christians, we often don't know what to say to an overworked mom like Carrie, the hitchhiker who asks for money, or kids like Leroy and Duante who don't have enough food. Too often, we say nothing. We do nothing. Jesus said, "You always have the poor with you" (Matt. 26:11), but that does not mean we shouldn't do what we can to help the poor.

Paul told the Thessalonians, "If anyone isn't willing to work, he should not eat" (2 Thess. 3:10). We have all heard this verse used to justify not giving to the needy, almost as if Carrie and Duante should "learn their lesson" the hard way. But the key word in the verse above is "willing." Paul is discouraging laziness, not giving Christ followers license to ignore the poor. In today's world, it is incredibly difficult for folks making minimum wage to support a family and provide the basics their children need in order to be healthy, especially when a single mom or dad is forced to work overtime just to put food on the table.

Are there people on welfare who are lazy? Of course. But I know a lot of rich people who are lazy too; they are just fortunate enough to have family money or other resources. However, for the vast majority of needy families, laziness is not the root issue.

Sweeping generalizations about the poor act like a cancer that destroys our compassion and generosity. When we judge or criticize the hitchhiking teenager or the beggar on the street corner, we are not loving them like Jesus would. Often we figure they don't deserve our help, but that is not the issue. After all, Jesus loves us and died for us even though *none* of us is deserving of it. How can we do any less?

I am just as guilty of judging the poor as anyone else. I've said things like, "Well, I'm sure they would just go buy some cigarettes or beer, and I don't want to enable an addict," or, "They have government help," or, "They can always go down to the homeless shelter." But here's the irony: We judge families who get government help while we fail to help those very same people. On top of that, we often advocate shutting down the very social programs that keep their kids from starving. If the government discontinued all welfare programs tomorrow, I'm not sure we would be ready, willing, or able to help all of the people in need in our communities.

We may tell ourselves, "It's not my problem. I have to take care of my own family." But if Christians are not responsible to care for the needy, who is?

It's a Matter of Resources

While it is important for us to care for impoverished kids by providing physical and financial resources, the best way to assist them is to help get the entire family out of poverty. In order for people to break the bonds of poverty, they need many resources—not just financial. Ruby K. Payne, in her book *A Framework for Understanding Poverty*, explains it this way:

Typically, poverty is thought of in terms of financial resources only. However, the reality is that *financial* resources, while extremely important, do not explain the differences in the success with which individuals leave poverty nor the reasons that many stay in poverty. The ability to leave poverty is more dependent on other resources than it is upon financial resources. Each of these resources plays a vital role in the success of an individual.

Emotional resources provide the stamina to withstand difficult and uncomfortable emotional situations and feelings. . . .

Mental resources are simply being able to process information and use it in daily living. If an individual can read, write, and compute, he/she has a decided advantage. . . .

Spiritual resources are the belief that help can be obtained from a higher power, that there is a purpose for living, and that worth and love are gifts from God. This is a powerful resource because the individual does not see him/herself as useless, but rather as capable and having worth and value.

Physical resources are having a body that works, that is capable and mobile. The individual can be self-sufficient.[4]

In addition, people in poverty need support systems, good role models, and knowledge of the "hidden rules" of the middle class. Many poor people, especially those whose families have been impoverished for generations, do not have these resources available to them, they don't know how to get them, and most do not even know they need them. As Christ followers, we need to help provide these resources in order to help children and their families get out of poverty, which will then decrease the number of orphaned, abandoned, and vulnerable children in our society. We are commanded to help orphans, but how much better it is if we can prevent children from becoming orphaned or abandoned in the first place.

Nationwide, there are many organizations—both Christian and secular—that provide the resources people in poverty need in order to get out of their situation. There are likely several such ministries in your area already. The problem is that these services are often underfunded, understaffed, and rely mainly on volunteer help, which often limits the number of people they can assist. If churches were to partner with these organizations and provide funding and volunteers, they could serve many more people and help break the cycle of poverty.

Many of these organizations need help from people like you. They need academic tutors who can teach a single mother to read. They are looking for accountants who can help families understand budgeting. They want administrative assistants to help an aspiring office worker learn how to type and do clerical work. They desperately need Christ followers from all walks of life and with all types of skills to serve as mentors and role models to help people gain the emotional and spiritual resources they need in order to create better lives for themselves and their children. Will you consider how you can help families move from poverty into hope? Will you ask God to give you a heart for the poor, then put feet to your prayers?

The "Two Shirts" Invitation

Scripture is forthright about God's heart for the poor. In Isaiah 58, God confronts His people about their fasting and other "religious" acts, while neglecting the poor among them: "Isn't the fast I choose . . . to share your bread with the hungry, to bring the poor and homeless into your house, to clothe the naked when you see him?" (Isa. 58:6–7).

How easy it is for us, just like the children of Israel, to get caught up in well-meaning religious acts like going to church, studying Scripture, and debating theology, while failing to live out the truths of God's Word. Throughout the Bible, more than 2,000 verses reference God's concern for the destitute and needy and His desire for us to have the same concern. Here are a few examples (all emphasis added):

- "The righteous *care about justice for the poor,* but the wicked have no such concern" (Prov. 29:7 NIV).
- "The one who oppresses the poor person insults his Maker, but one who *is kind to the needy* honors Him" (Prov. 14:31).
- "If there is a poor man among your brothers in any of the towns of the land that the LORD your God is giving you, *do not be hardhearted* or tightfisted toward your poor brother. Rather *be openhanded* and freely lend him whatever he needs" (Deut. 15:7–8 NIV).
- "He who is *kind to the poor* lends to the LORD, and he will reward him for what he has done" (Prov. 19:17 NIV).
- "The one who shuts his ears to the cry of the poor will himself also *call out and not be answered*" (Prov. 21:13).

These verses emphasize our heart attitude toward the poor, which has direct implications on our personal relationship with the Lord. It's not as simple as leaving a nice tip or giving more to charity, though that is important. As the American church, we need a fundamental change of heart. When we see a homeless person on the side of the street, instead of assuming he is lazy and his homelessness is his own fault, we should be reminded of our own neediness and dependence on God. What if God's attitude toward us had been the same as our attitude toward the poor? What if the Lord had shut His ears? What if He was not kind to us? What if He had been hard-hearted instead? What if we called out and He didn't answer?

It is believed that Martin Luther's last written words were, "We are beggars: this is true."[5] The reality is that each of us is impoverished without God. Not only that, we were spiritually dead. But God did hear us; He did extend kindness and offer mercy when we didn't deserve it.

When our heart attitudes begin to shift from judgment to compassion, our actions will follow—not out of guilt or obligation, but as a joyful response to the gospel and its work in our own lives. Scripture paints a beautiful and convicting picture of the generosity that should characterize a Christ follower's life (all emphasis added):

- "If you *offer yourself to the hungry,* and satisfy the afflicted one, then your light will shine in the darkness, and your night will be like noonday" (Isa. 58:10).
- "Go, sell your belongings and *give to the poor,* and you will have treasure in heaven. Then come, follow Me" (Matt. 19:21).
- "Speak up, judge righteously, and *defend the cause of the oppressed and needy"* (Prov. 31:9).
- "Sell your possessions and *give to the poor.* Make money-bags for yourselves that won't grow old, an inexhaustible

treasure in heaven, where no thief comes near and no moth destroys" (Luke 12:33).

- "When you host a banquet, *invite those who are poor, maimed, lame, or blind*" (Luke 14:13).

The overwhelming message here is simple: As Jesus' disciples, we are called to live sacrificially so we can give generously. A "poor = lazy" mindset blinds us to the needs of vulnerable children. These kids did not choose poverty, but they live in it every day, and many have no hope of getting out of it. If we claim to care about orphaned and vulnerable children, we can't dismiss the poverty that is rampant both on the other side of the world and at our doorstep. Regardless of our political stance—conservative or liberal—we are all commanded to share liberally, particularly with at-risk and needy children.

More than just writing a check, God's Word challenges us to invite the poor and needy into our everyday lives. While this sacrificial living will likely look different for each of us, it will require giving up some of our creature comforts, much like John the Baptist challenged the crowds: "The one who has two shirts must share with someone who has none, and the one who has food must do the same" (Luke 3:11).

Poverty is not necessarily an issue to solve; it is an opportunity to serve. As we go through each day, our hearts' cry should be, *Lord, where would You have me give, serve, and invest myself to bring hope to the poor?* I challenge you to apply the "two shirts" principle to your life—not out of guilt, but out of joyful obedience.

Thatch Huts and My Own Poverty

"Hey Johnny, what do you think about those huts?" My friend Tendai nodded at the thatch houses scattered across the

Ethiopian countryside. His words hung in the air, and I didn't know quite what to say. Many of the tiny straw shanties looked like they could collapse any minute.

"Uhhh, are you asking me if I could live in one?" I chuckled.

"Yeah," he smiled. Then, in his rich and beautiful Zimbabwean accent, he said, "When I was a kid, my home looked just like that."

As we stood there in awkward silence, my joke didn't seem so funny anymore. Tendai, who now lives in the United States, pointed to an older man sitting in front of his hut. "You see that guy? He only has one thing to worry about today—food. Me and you, we have rush hour traffic, work deadlines, cell phone bills, car payments, mortgages, insurance, college tuition . . ." His next words radically changed how I view people living in poverty: "It's a hard life, but in many ways it's a good life. You can be poor and be happy."

Could people really be poor and happy? That thought didn't sit well with my Western tendency to pity guys like Tendai because he grew up without the Disney Channel, Xbox, and Fruit Loops. Sure, he had a thatch roof over his head and food to eat, but he missed so much as a kid. But did I have something to learn from my brother's humility, contentment, and reliance on God?

During my years as a pastor, I've heard countless presentations with the premise, "The poor starving kids in Africa need your help," and that is true. But in that moment with Tendai, I realized that as much as those kids do desperately need food, I need God to open my eyes to see the desperate, prideful condition of my own heart. How despicable of me to look down on the guy sitting in the dirt by his thatch hut as if he were less valuable, less intelligent, less worth my time, less human. Looking back, this impoverished Ethiopian man taught me more about the poverty of my own heart than any seminary professor ever did.

People living in extreme poverty need food, clothing, and shelter to survive another day. We cannot dismiss these very real physical needs. But we also must bring them hope. If we as Christ followers do not truly care about people in poverty, we can never bring hope to their desperate lives. We may offer them all kinds of money, since we live in the wealthiest country in the world, but more than anything, the poor need hope.

Wess Stafford, President of Compassion International, witnessed this reality firsthand growing up as a missionary kid. He says it far better than I ever could: "I learned in my childhood in Africa that a child may be born into poverty, but poverty is never born in a child. The worst aspects of poverty are not the deplorable outward conditions but rather the erosion and eventual destruction of hope, and therefore, dreams."[6]

Poverty is not just a lack of food. It's a culture of hopelessness, a culture that produces orphans. If children grow up without families, the chances of them breaking out of poverty are slim to none. If these destitute kids live to be adults, they will most likely bring children into the world and into a culture of poverty. It's a vicious cycle.

If we say that we truly care about orphaned and vulnerable children, we must care about poverty and those living in it. Poverty produces more orphaned and vulnerable children than any other factor. Many children are abandoned, left at orphanages, or forced to enter the American foster care system not because their parents have died, but because their mother and father are too poor to care for them. Poverty colors a child's world with fear, uncertainty, and desperation. It robs kids of hope and destroys their futures.

Changing the Music

What is it like to see poverty through an orphan's eyes? I'll never forget how this came alive to me at a training event about adoption. I was expecting a PowerPoint lecture, but the speaker began quite simply, "I want to ask you to do something a little bit unconventional. Please close your eyes and relax." Soft classical music filled the room.

"In just a moment," she continued, "I'm going to ask you to open your eyes and write down the first word that comes to mind when you see the picture on the screen." A photo of a beautiful Hawaiian beach flashed on the screen. Most of us wrote down words like "peaceful," "relaxing," "vacation," and "fun." Moving on, she said, "Now, close your eyes again, and let's repeat this exercise." The theme from the killer shark movie *Jaws* blasted through the speakers, and it startled me a bit. I opened my eyes and saw the same picture as before. This time, the words that came to mind were "blood," "killer," "danger," and "fear."

"All of us have a soundtrack for life," the speaker explained. "And that music influences everything we see and experience. Kids from loving, stable homes, with a bed to sleep in at night and food on the table, look at the world and see fun, adventure, and opportunity. But children whose daily reality is hunger, abuse, and neglect look at the same world and see threats, danger, abandonment, and hopelessness."

Children in poverty don't just need food; they need new music. I am not a fan of "Sunday school answers" when it comes to complex global issues—and poverty may be the most significant problem in our world today—but with every fiber of my being, I believe that the gospel is the only true answer to poverty. It is the only soundtrack of lasting hope, the only way to break this generational cycle.

We can't just feed kids' souls and leave their bellies empty, but we can't just put food in their bellies and stop there either. We must do both. Books like *Too Small to Ignore* by Wess Stafford and *When Helping Hurts* by Steve Corbett and Brian Fikkert offer great practical resources to walk through as a mission or outreach team before going out to serve. Whether we're going across town to help a kid like Duante or across the world to minister to kids in an orphanage, we need wisdom to know how to respond to the poor in genuine compassion and love, not just pity or a desire to rescue. We must be strategic about our approach to working with those in poverty, remembering that they don't just need money. They also need hope. We must be willing to study the issues and search for lasting solutions that will help break the generational cycle of poverty.

There are no easy answers. As a pastor, one of the toughest situations I've been faced with is knowing what to say to the family who asks for help when it's obvious they are trying to prey on the church's generosity rather than living responsibly themselves. I have wrestled many a night about what to do in these situations, because I can't get rid of the image of the three innocent kids sitting in the backseat of their car. I know these kids will suffer if the church walks away.

To be honest, this has been the toughest chapter of all to write. I am not smart enough to offer novel answers or global solutions, but that is not my goal. However, I do know this: Poverty produces orphaned and vulnerable children.

I've seen in my own heart and that of many other Christians that our mind-set toward the poor is often demeaning and belittling. We see ourselves as "better," even when we don't mean to. This is a gross misunderstanding of the gospel and the generosity Christ has offered us through the cross.

I don't know if we will ever eradicate poverty, but we can ask God to examine our heart attitudes toward the poor. We can confess where we have been wrong. And we can ask God to move our hearts with true compassion that calls us to a lifestyle of sacrifice and generosity toward vulnerable children.

A Variety of Methods

There is no perfect method for helping people in poverty. The needs vary from place to place, as do the resources available to help the poor. However, a number of churches and parachurch ministries are helping the impoverished all around the world in many different ways.

One noteworthy ministry that reaches out to impoverished children domestically is Safe Families for Children. While working with a foster care ministry in Chicago, founder Dave Anderson became deeply burdened to help families with children who are in a time of crisis but simply don't have the resources or family support to provide the basic necessities for their children. These families find themselves in a position where if someone doesn't step in to help care for their children for a short period of time, the kids will be forced into foster care.

Seeing how such crises can destroy families and tear kids away from their parents, Anderson began recruiting Christian families who would be willing to open up their homes and host these children, allowing parents to get on their feet again while recovering from sickness, completing a rehabilitation program, serving a short jail sentence for a misdemeanor, or finding housing or a job.

Host families have the opportunity to tangibly minister to the children as well as to their parents. By doing so, these concerned Christ followers actually enter into the family's poverty—rather than just writing a check or giving some cans of food—and see with their own eyes that many of these families are not lazy, but desperate for help. Anderson describes this outreach as "the purest form of biblical hospitality" and challenges other Christ followers and churches around the country to implement a similar model.

The Church at Osage Hills in Osage Beach, Missouri, is doing something to help kids like Duante and Leroy who don't get adequate food when they're not in school. In partnership with the Central Missouri Food Bank, they provide "Buddy Packs" for kids in need. Any child who qualifies for free or reduced meals and has parental permission gets a bag full of nonperishable, easy-to-fix, nutritious food each Friday to help get them through the weekend. In order to help preserve kids' pride and dignity, the Buddy Packs are placed inside the kids' backpacks while they are out of the classroom. Without this food, many kids would go hungry in this region where more than 50 percent of children receive free and reduced lunches.

In addition to leading the push to feed hungry kids, Osage Hills has made the entire community aware of the needs of the region's vulnerable children. Through the church's efforts, the area hospital, local grocery stores, other churches, and many other businesses and individuals in the community have stepped forward with money, food, resources, and volunteers for the Buddy Pack program. Because of the commitment and actions of one church, an entire community is now involved in caring for vulnerable children.

Internationally, even more than domestically, the challenge of addressing poverty and truly helping is a daunting task. A microfinance model has recently been implemented as a highly successful self-sustainable approach that offers hope to break the cycle of poverty. As opposed to a free handout, which lasts for only a short while and creates dependence on U.S. aid, microfinance teaches business and trade skills, encouraging creativity, ingenuity, and independence.

Microloans are offered to families or individuals to help fund business endeavors and give those in extreme poverty an opportunity to work their way out of poverty with a sustainable private business. It could be as simple as growing coffee beans, baking bread, selling eggs, or making jewelry, pottery, or clothing. The list of possibilities is endless, depending on the community, climate, and available resources. Through this model, a family is given a loan, coached in how to use the money, and then held accountable for how it is used. When their business becomes self-sustaining, they pay the interest-free loan back, and it is used to help another family.

Again, not all of those who live in poverty are lazy—many barely have enough resources to put food in their children's mouths, never mind having the funds to consider starting a business. They have no money to invest in buying something as simple as a sewing machine, a plow, or a flock of chickens, and the current banking structure and unstable economy of many countries rule out the possibility of financial investment. Through microfinance, however, families are able to begin to make modest—and stable—incomes. As a result, they are better able to care for their children by providing basic nutrition, shelter, and clothing, rather than being forced to leave them at an orphanage or abandon them in the hopes they will be adopted.

Poverty is not a social justice issue for governments to figure out. It is an invitation to each one of us to reach out in humble gratitude for how God has rescued us, not forgetting our own poverty and desperate need for Him. If we truly want to break the cycle of poverty and hopelessness, we must start with our own hearts.

What You Can Do

ANYONE can evaluate your lifestyle and budget and ask God to open your eyes to the needy people around you that you can bless. Make an intentional decision to say "no" to something each month so that you can give generously. Talk to your family about this and make sure everyone understands why you are giving up the opportunity to eat out and stay home for sandwiches. Then write a check for the amount you would have spent on the meal and pray over it as a family before doing something tangible with the money. You might want to take the cash, purchase food, and distribute it to a few homeless people in your community.

Domestically, MANY can financially support and volunteer to help with a local Buddy Pack program. Call your local school district to see if this outreach is provided to their students; ask them who provides this service—a food bank, a church, a local nonprofit—and how you can get involved. MANY can also begin a ministry at your church to provide backpacks with age- and gender-appropriate items for children entering the foster system. Many children come into the system with only the clothes on their backs due to the poverty in which they live. Connect with your local foster care agency so that when children are brought into the foster system, you can supply them with needed items like toiletries, socks, and underwear, and fun items like cars, coloring books, and dolls.

Internationally, MANY can partner with an organization that supports microfinance by buying products such jewelry, bags, or clothing. Consider hosting a party, much like a jewelry or Tupperware party, and encourage your friends to buy these micro-finance items. For a few examples, check out www.rahabsrope.com or www.hopeinternational.org.

A FEW can research Safe Families for Children (www. safe-families.org) and talk to local agencies about starting Safe Families in your area or becoming involved if it has already been started. A FEW can also help start a Buddy Pack program in your area if one does not currently exist. Contact the local school district to find out what the need is, talk with your church leaders, and consider what your church can do to help. Also call your local food bank, tell them your church is interested in partnering with them to help feed hungry kids, and suggest they look into what agencies like the Central Missouri Food Bank are doing to help feed kids through Buddy Packs (www.sharefoodbringhope.org).

CHAPTER 6

To Love Is to Risk

Orphans and Foster Care

So what do you want to do about Ben?" Silence hung heavy in the air as the social worker leaned across the plastic Burger King table to hear my response. Several weeks earlier, Ben had joined our family through foster care, and we had high hopes of adopting him as our own child. We were his fourteenth foster home over the course of his short life, and we had determined to be his "forever family."

However, once Ben moved in, significant behavioral issues began to surface that we had not been aware of. Meanwhile, our two adopted children were struggling with significant attachment issues. To top it off, Beth's mom was battling terminal cancer. It was not exactly the life I'd always imagined. As a husband, father, and the leader of our household, I begged God for wisdom as I considered Beth's vulnerable state, our children's challenges, and Ben's unique needs.

The echo of children's laughter floated in from the Burger King play area, and in that moment, I knew exactly what I *wanted* to do. I wanted to wave a magic wand and solve everything. I wanted to "fix" all of Ben's problems so he would be a perfect fit for our family. I wanted to rewind his story and protect him from the physical and sexual abuse that had robbed him of childhood. I wanted to reprogram his emotional state and show him that our family really was a safe place. I wanted to see Ben laugh, to free him from the anger and fear that crippled him. I wanted to play tackle football with him in the backyard, to take him on camping trips, to teach him how to play baseball, and to show him how to treat a woman with respect.

I wanted the chaos and craziness in our family to disappear. I wanted to fix all of our problems so that we could be the family that Ben needed. I wanted to cure James and Xiaoli's attachment challenges so they could be the perfect brother and sister. I wanted to heal my mother-in-law of her terminal cancer so she could be the perfect grandma Ben never had. I wanted to rescue my wife from the emotional torment of watching her mother die a slow and horrible death. Yet, I found myself—a grown man—completely helpless to do anything.

Is Love All You Need?

"The toughest job you'll ever love." I never joined the Peace Corps, but their slogan hits close to home. Foster care can be one of the most challenging, yet rewarding, experiences you will ever encounter. To welcome forgotten kids into your home and love them as your own children showcases the heart of Jesus in a powerful way.

However, foster parenting is also emotionally taxing, physically demanding, and downright messy. It's certainly not for the faint of heart. In most cases, foster kids carry the wounds of abuse and neglect. In some terrible cases, children have been beaten or even raped by their own family members. They've been locked in closets, left outside in the cold, deprived of food . . . the list of horrors goes on.

Far from a safe place, their families are a living nightmare. This is the height of evil—when the family, which God created as a safe place for children to be loved and nurtured, becomes a place of torture, neglect, and cruelty. The very hands that should reach out in a loving embrace lash out in anger instead.

These children are broken and hurting. It is not surprising, then, that many suffer from significant psychological, emotional, and behavioral challenges. And there are no easy answers, except to walk away. But we dare not, because Jesus Himself said, "Let the children come to me. Don't stop them! For the Kingdom of Heaven belongs to those who are like these children" (Matt. 19:14 NLT).

As Jesus' followers, we neglect the work of His kingdom when we dismiss foster care because it is a difficult and politically laden issue. But engaging our hearts to examine foster care takes God-sized courage, love, and wisdom. Our own story is certainly less than perfect.

As Beth and I began to research orphaned and vulnerable children within the U.S., we were shocked to discover that more than 400,000 children are part of the foster care system.[1] Their parents may be incarcerated, deceased, sick, or homeless, but whatever the reason, they are clearly not able to care for their children at the present time. In such cases, the state steps in to provide interim care for these kids through foster families. If parental rights are terminated, foster children become available for adoption.

And this is how we met Ben. God really began to tug on our hearts about welcoming another child into our family by adopting through the foster care system. And so we obeyed. (I may be hardheaded, but I'm learning.) As we met with caseworkers and helped Ben get settled in, our entire family felt God opening our hearts to love and care for this precious little boy. Ben's social worker had described him as shy, sweet, and eager to please, but as significant mental health issues began to emerge, we begged God for wisdom. In the midst of this turmoil, the phone rang. It was Beth's mother, who had been fighting aggressive lung cancer. "I'm done, Beth. I can't do this anymore. I'm done fighting. I'm done with chemo. I'm done."

In that moment, everything changed. For months, we had been hoping, praying, and begging God to heal Beth's mother. But as the tragic reality set in of her final days, she desperately needed our care. She lived five hours away, so Beth experienced long nights of driving, sleeping on her couch, giving meds, sitting by her bedside, and enjoying a few precious memories as her mother's life slipped away.

This shift of energy and focus only added to the chaos of our home and our own personal crisis. Ben's chaotic history demanded a stable home in order for him to successfully transition into an adoptive family. As much as we wanted to be that family for Ben, Beth and I began to realize that we were stretched beyond our limit. We just couldn't give Ben the attention and care he needed in order to thrive. Our family was fragile, and since we already had two adopted children with special needs, I began to wonder about our responsibility to not put James and Xiaoli at undue risk.

As a husband and a father, I knew I had to weigh the cost. I knew that, realistically, our family's time and energy to invest in Ben's life was very limited, due to the current demands with Beth's mom. I knew that the timing was not right and that if we proceeded with the adoption, we were taking risks that could be dangerous to the well-being of Ben and our entire family. And it broke my heart. Ben desperately needed a family to be fully invested in him for the next year, and we were not that family.

Sitting in the cramped Burger King booth, I fought back the tears as I turned to the social worker and said, "If he stays with us, we will not be able to offer him what he needs. How do we make this transition?"

She looked at me and simply said, "Let's go to your house."

I couldn't believe it would end like this after the months of prayers, tears, and the firm conviction that God had brought Ben to our family. One minute I was sipping a Diet Coke in Burger King, the next I was packing up Ben's clothes and toys while the social worker tried to explain to him what was happening. From the bedroom upstairs, I heard him crying, "I want this to be my family! I want this to be my family!"

Ben screamed hysterically as we loaded his things in the social worker's car and helped him into the front seat. His tear-stained face looked up at mine, and the desperation in his eyes cut my heart open.

I wanted to hold Ben in my arms one last time. I desperately wanted to tell him that we loved him and that it was going to be okay, that his forever family was out there waiting for him. But I had no words. I had no promise. Honestly, I didn't know what would happen to him. I have never felt more like a failure in my entire life.

When I walked back inside, James and Xiaoli were standing and staring, their faces white as a sheet. They both had tears in their eyes. I knew they must have been thinking, *If I'm bad, will you send me away too?*

This was the hardest decision Beth and I have ever made. There wasn't a dry eye in the house that day, and even now, I can't think about Ben without choking up. We had hopes and dreams for "Ben Carr." We went into the process prayerfully, thinking that the transition would go just as smoothly as our adoptions of James and Xiaoli, but it turned out to be one of the most hurtful and emotionally draining experiences that we have ever been through.

Adoption is a faith journey—from beginning to end—especially when adopting an older child who brings a significant history. Even in the best of circumstances, that "history" is traumatic, and no amount of love can erase those memories.

Foster care is risky. Adoption is risky. Love itself is always risky.

However, while adoption is not for every family, there is a family for every child who needs to be adopted. We were not the family for Ben. I can still see that Ford Focus driving away. Ben's screams still echo in my ears. How I wish I could have grabbed my GPS, run after the car, and handed it to the social worker with the address of his adoptive family already entered in.

But I couldn't.

Throwing the Baby out with the Bathwater

Seven years is the average age of kids entering the foster care system.[2] Many of these children have seen more craziness in their few short years than you or I could ever imagine. The foster care system aims to provide these vulnerable kids with a stable, safe home environment, and ultimately, "permanency with caring parents."[3] Adoption is one answer, but only about one in every four foster kids is free to be adopted, which is around 100,000 children.

The remaining 300,000 children have been removed from their homes because of abuse, violence, homelessness, illness, or incarceration. Nearly half of these kids have a case plan goal of being reunited with their families one day, 4 percent hope to live with another relative, 6 percent hope to be emancipated, and 4 percent hope to obtain a legal guardian. For some kids, case plans have not been established, but only 8 percent have a goal of long-term foster care.[4]

It is estimated that about 65 percent of kids who leave foster care go back to live with a parent, relative, or guardian, 11 percent are emancipated, 20 percent are adopted, and 3 percent have "other outcomes."[5]

These "other outcomes" may include running away or death. That's 8,000 kids a year the system fails. These kids are vulnerable, hurting, and desperate. In many cases, they are drawn into drugs, prostitution, or gang life. Some even take their own life.

Foster care is not a cakewalk. It's a flawed government system that attempts to help children in crisis. These kids typically enter the foster care system because of a complaint filed with Child Protective Services by a concerned neighbor, teacher, or friend. A social worker investigates the report and determines whether the child's home situation puts him or her at risk of physical or psychological harm.

Children may be taken into the custody of the state for a number of reasons. Many kids are removed due to suspected abuse or neglect. Some children end up in foster care simply because their parents are not able to provide proper care. This is especially a struggle among single parents who may be hospitalized or incapacitated because of medical issues. Parents may be temporarily homeless because of financial problems or incarceration. Whatever the case may be, the common denominator here is that parents cannot provide the basics of food, clothing, and shelter for their child at the moment.

Children officially "enter" the system by being brought before a family court judge within twenty-four hours of removal from their home in order to determine if there is just cause for the state to assume custody. Some kids are returned home because suspected abuse or neglect cannot be substantiated to the court's satisfaction. When the court does rule for a child to be placed in foster care, the state assumes legal responsibility for the child's welfare. This includes deciding where and with whom the child lives.

In most cases, parents are given a plan and the help needed to make appropriate changes in their lives so they can safely parent their children again. Often, parents try again and fail, and kids end up bouncing back and forth between their home and foster care multiple times.

The foster care system is often messy. Attempts to help these kids can sometimes hurt them. Take the case of Sally, for example. Sally was removed from her home when she was seven years old because her mother's boyfriend was abusing her. She was placed in the Smith's home for foster care, and as she adjusted, she began to feel safe and happy. Eight months later, Sally's birth mom met the requirements to regain custody. Sally felt torn, because she loved her foster family, but she was excited to live with her mom again.

However, Sally's mom didn't really have her life together. As her mother battled drug addiction, eight-year-old Sally was left to cook, clean, and care for herself. When the social worker became aware of this, Sally was once again placed in the foster care system. The Smith family had another foster child by that point, so Sally was shuffled to a different home. The new foster family wasn't like the Smiths. They treated Sally more like a slave than a child, forcing her to do all the housework while their own kids watched TV or played video games. Sally reacted behaviorally. She didn't feel understood, loved, or cared for. The social worker claimed it wasn't a good "fit" and moved Sally to a third home.

Sally has lived with four different families over the last two years. Who knows how many more families she will be part of before she goes home, if she ever does go home. The life of a foster child is tough, uncertain, and scary.

When you hear stories of kids being placed with five, ten, or twenty different foster families, it's no exaggeration. There is nothing healthy about this for a child. Unfortunately, in some cases, it's the best the state system has to offer.

In situations where parents show that they are consistently irresponsible and unfit to provide care, the judge will likely sever parental rights. These children become legally free for adoption, meaning that you or I could legally adopt them. "Free" doesn't refer to costs, although most families pay little to nothing out of pocket to adopt from the foster system. It refers to the fact that these children are now legally orphaned.

Foster care has often been criticized because of the instability and change it brings to kids' lives during the critical years of their development. But when a child's home is riddled with abuse, addiction, and neglect, it cannot be a safe place to stay.

So do we work in a flawed system for the sake of the kids or should we throw the proverbial baby out with the bathwater? I will be the first to admit that foster care is not ideal. It is a substitute, but it is a substitute that attempts to protect children and place them in safe, loving families.

My experience tells me that there are two main reasons that more Christians are not providing homes for children in foster care. One reason is Big Brother. When you foster a child, you are inviting the government into your home. The second reason is the emotional expense of seeing a child leave your home and return to an environment of possible abuse and neglect.

Hello Big Brother, Goodbye Spanking

Like it or not, when you choose to become a foster family or adopt through the state, you are welcoming Big Brother right into your house. You're inviting him to pull up a chair at the dinner table, to watch TV, to tag along to the kids' ball games, and to piggyback on your vacation.

Not surprisingly, many Christians view the government's regulations and requirements for becoming a foster parent as intrusive and controlling. But the reality is this: Since the state carries the legal burden to care for foster children, they also make the rules. If you want to reach out in love to these kids, you will have to submit to the authority of the state. As Paul reminds us in Romans 13:1, "Everyone must submit to the governing authorities." The idea of outside control is not appealing to many of us, but it's one of those "necessary evils" we must wrestle through to minister to kids in foster care.

To be quite honest, the majority of state regulations ensure a child's safety and really do make sense. For example, our family was required to install fire extinguishers and smoke alarms. Our home had to be set up so children of different genders would not be sharing a bedroom. Most of us would agree that these are wise moves for any family—foster care or not.

But one regulation that many Christians take issue with is spanking. Foster parents are not allowed to use any form of corporal punishment in their discipline. Some well-meaning pastors have warned their congregations against becoming foster parents because of this restriction.

In many biblically based models of child rearing, spanking is a central tenet of discipline. Scripture clearly expresses this idea: "Foolishness is tangled up in the heart of a youth; the rod of discipline will drive it away from him" (Prov. 22:15). "A rod of correction imparts wisdom, but a youth left to himself is a disgrace to his mother" (Prov. 29:15). These verses are pretty straightforward—"the rod of correction" plays an important part in biblical parenting. However, before we make sweeping statements about spanking, it is important to consider a child's history and the context for discipline.

Many foster children carry painful memories of being mistreated, beaten, and abused. I will never forget the day a foster child shared with me the gory details of being hit in the head with a baseball bat. With victims of this type of violence, any type of physical touch—even a hug or roughhousing—can trigger flashbacks from the past. Spanking, in particular, can re-traumatize a child and activate fear, defensiveness, anger, and self-protection. Far from teaching a lesson and encouraging obedience, corporal punishment can actually reinforce a child's distrust of authority figures. When working with hurting kids, spanking may cut off the safe relationship you are trying so desperately to build.

An expert researcher in this area, Dr. Karyn Purvis warns parents that, for children of trauma, spanking is the absolute worst thing you can do to address negative behavior, as it only heightens their anxiety and reactivity.[6] Research has found that children who have lived as victims of abuse actually experience changes in the physical and chemical makeup of their brain as a result.[7]

Wisdom is needed here. First of all, once you have signed a commitment with the state saying that you will not spank, your integrity is on the line. Secondly, a foster parent is not technically the child's parent, but instead a temporary caregiver while the parent is absent. Therefore, the biblical premise of parents spanking their children does not hold true. But let's push this argument a little further.

What about kids who have been adopted? In this case, parents are no longer bound by the regulations of the foster system and are free to discipline in ways that obviously do not constitute abuse. But before you pull out the paddle, stop and think. I hesitate to advocate spanking children who have been adopted, especially children adopted at older ages or who are coming from traumatic or abusive experiences. Spanking may produce immediate results in correcting a child's behavior, but could miss the goal of constructive discipline. Any form of correction we use should facilitate a child's growth and character development and ultimately draw their hearts into a loving relationship.

When I first spanked our oldest daughter, Heather, who was born to us, our relationship had a history of unconditional love, trust, and safety. As much as a three-year-old could understand, she knew that Mommy and Daddy loved her. James came into our lives at four years old and Xiaoli was almost six, each possibly carrying a history of neglect and abuse. To spank them could reinforce traumatic histories.

Dr. James Dobson, former President of Focus on the Family, is widely known as an outspoken proponent of biblical spanking. His insights offer a fresh perspective, particularly as we consider children whose history we do not know, who come from abusive backgrounds, or who are adopted at older ages:

> Ultimately, the key to competent parenthood is in being able to get behind the eyes of your child, seeing what he sees and feeling what he feels. When he is lonely, he needs your company. When he is defiant, he needs your help in controlling his impulses. When he is afraid, he needs the security of your embrace. When he is curious, he needs your patient instruction. When he is happy, he needs to share his laughter and joy with those he loves. Thus, the parent who intuitively comprehends his child's feelings is in a position to respond appropriately and meet the needs that are apparent. And at this point, raising healthy children becomes a highly developed art, requiring

the greatest wisdom, patience, devotion, and love
that God has given to us.[8]

What would it look like for you to get behind the eyes of your child? Believe me, it changes everything in the way you see your child and respond to their disruptive behavior. One particular Scripture stands out to me that Paul penned, "Fathers, don't stir up anger in your children, but bring them up in the training and instruction of the Lord" (Eph. 6:4). If we spank a child with whom we do not have a foundation of love and trust, or a child from an abusive background, we may very well be stirring up anger in them.

As Christians, our foundation for parenting is obviously Scripture. I am not saying that Dr. Purvis or Dr. Dobson trump the writer of Proverbs, but I am saying that a holistic approach is needed. A mentor of mine, Willy Rice, often said in his sermons, "Rules without relationship equals rebellion." Be careful in your discipline not to fall prey to rule-based parenting. If you do not take time to build a relationship with your kids—particularly those who join your family through foster care or adoption—attempts to discipline will likely backfire.

When a child is placed into your home, you will have to develop a relationship and establish rules. Finding the balance is incredibly difficult. If you have a relationship without rules, a foster child will run over you. If you have rules without a relationship, he or she will likely rebel.

We must seek out godly wisdom to navigate the challenges of the foster care system, while still guiding children in a loving, constructive manner. It is not always as simple as pulling out the paddle.

How Will I Let Them Go?

Like any relationship, becoming a foster parent requires a significant emotional commitment. But unlike giving birth to a child, you welcome a foster child into your home knowing that, at some point, you will probably have to say goodbye. A child's stay in one foster home may range from twenty-four hours to a couple of months to several years. Of kids who exit the foster care system, roughly 46 percent were in the system for less than a year, 36 percent were in the system for one to three years, and 17 percent were in the system for more than three years.[9]

Thankfully, many foster kids eventually have the opportunity to live with a family member again. They may go back to their own parents, a grandparent, or an aunt or uncle. This is always the end goal whenever the child is not at risk of harm. In a broken world, living at home is not always possible, but as foster parents, we should always desire for the situation to be resolved so that foster children can rejoin their biological families. But family isn't always an option. Tragically, nearly 2,000 foster children age out of the foster system each year. They turn eighteen, exit the system, and have no place to call home.[10]

Whether your foster child moves back home, is transferred to another foster family, ends up in a group home, or ages out of the system, 80 percent of the time saying "goodbye" is inevitable. Many parents wonder, *How can we really love a child like our own if we know it's only temporary? How will we ever let our foster child go without our hearts being torn to shreds? How can we be okay with our kid moving back into a potentially abusive home situation?*

I have heard it over and over again. I've even wrestled through these questions myself. C. S. Lewis addressed this fear well when he wrote, "To love at all is to be vulnerable. Love anything and your heart will be wrung and possibly broken."[11]

To love is to risk. Opening your home to a foster kid will be emotionally difficult. It's inconvenient. It's hard. It's messy. It's exhausting. I guarantee it.

But all too often, selfishness keeps us from taking care of these children. Somewhere along the way, in our concern for an easy, happy, comfortable life, we may be missing the heart of the gospel—to seek and save the lost, to reach out to the forgotten and the oppressed, to love sacrificially, and to pour our lives out so that others can catch a glimpse of Jesus.

If the only reason we refuse to get involved in foster care is because "it is too hard emotionally" or "we can't handle saying goodbye," we may need to repent of self-absorption. We must ask the question: Do we truly love our neighbor as we love ourselves? What if a foster child is the "neighbor" that God has brought into our path to love?

The life of a foster child is tough. Being removed from home and sent to live with strangers, often with very little notice, can be quite traumatic. Like no other time in their lives, these kids desperately need Christ followers to "be there" for them. You might think that you could never foster Sally for six months and then watch her go back to an environment where she might be abused again. But think about it this way: *Sally is going to be in the foster system for those six months whether she is in your home or not.* We have all heard horror stories of corrupt and abusive foster parents. These stories are the exception, not the rule, but kids in these homes end up with a double dose of abuse and neglect, and this is a tragedy. The body of Christ must recruit stable, safe foster families for these children.

Again, becoming a foster parent is not for everyone, but instead of seeing the temporary and uncertain nature of fostering as an obstacle, we must consider it an opportunity to invest. Each day we have with foster children is an opportunity to live out the gospel by loving them in tangible ways, even (and especially) when they don't deserve it. We can give them the gift of being part of a safe, nurturing family. We have the ability to rock their world by the way we notice, listen, and care, rather than brushing them aside.

You Don't Have to Be a Superhero

Born to a mother with severe psychological issues, Kala didn't have the ideal childhood. She never knew her biological father. When he found out his girlfriend was pregnant, he ran. Kala's birth mother tried to raise her, but she was faced with overwhelming challenges. At the age of six, Kala was placed in a foster home. At nine, she was adopted.

During one of our church's Orphan Sundays, I had the opportunity to interview Kala. Her story is incredible. Now in her early twenties, Kala is a follower of Jesus and actively involved in local college ministry. She is approachable, smart, witty, self-confident, and pretty.

"I would not be who I am today without the love, patience, and support of my adoptive family," Kala shared with the congregation. "As a scared, shy, and confused nine-year-old, I didn't really know what to expect in a family. All I had ever known was chaos. But today, as I look back, I can't tell you how grateful I am for my mom and my dad. You have laughed with me, cried with me, and been there for me when I needed you most." There wasn't a dry eye in the room.

I wanted to recognize Kala's parents by asking them to stand and having everyone clap, but I couldn't because her dad is confined to a wheelchair. He is a wonderful adoptive father, and he is a paraplegic. You don't have to be "perfect" to foster or adopt a child. Kala's parents certainly are not superheroes; they are a normal, everyday family. Yes, they are a family with significant challenges, but they had big hearts to love a hurting little girl. This family was willing to accept Kala into their family with all of the physical and emotional bumps and bruises she had been given by a life that she did not choose. Their willingness to sacrifice, to be patient, and to unselfishly love has made a huge impact on Kala's life.

Ministering to children in foster care is challenging, but it is a privilege. It is an opportunity to provide a safe place and change a hurting kid's life. These forgotten children are precious to Jesus. He weeps to see them abused, misunderstood, and often headed down a destructive life path. When you become a foster parent or adopt a child, you are doing Jesus stuff. You are giving the opportunity for someone to have a new life, a new identity, and a new family.

To be honest, Kala's story is not the norm. Many children do not have the blessing of such godly, loving adoptive parents. That makes it all the more important for Christians and churches to actually make a difference in the foster care system.

We must open our eyes. We have a responsibility to educate our congregations about God's heart for orphaned, vulnerable, and forgotten children. Our congregations must realize the theological implications of adoption. Russell Moore, Dan Cruver, Daniel Bennett, Tony Merida, and Rick Morton are all authors who have successfully tackled this area. I encourage you to read their books.[12]

We must delve into the plight of foster kids in our own communities. How many children are in the foster care system in your state? How many are waiting for a foster family? How many are available for adoption? Have those numbers ever been shared from the pulpit of your church?

We must prayerfully consider whether God is calling our families to open our hearts and our homes to a foster child. To dismiss this issue for "more important things" is dangerous. Jesus gives a somber warning to those who refuse to care about the hurting and needy:

> For I was hungry and you gave Me nothing to eat; I was thirsty and you gave Me nothing to drink; I was a stranger and you didn't take Me in; I was naked and you didn't clothe Me. . . . Whatever you did not do for one of the least of these, you did not do for Me. (Matt. 25:42–43, 45)

What You Can Do

ANYONE can look for families in your church or community who are foster parents and reach out to encourage them. You can invite them to your home, provide a meal for the family, and let them know that you support them.

MANY can consider becoming a respite care worker for foster families. Respite workers are trained and screened to make sure they are ready to help care for kids with physical and emotional special needs. The respite time could be a couple of hours to a couple of weeks according to the need and the situation that arises in the foster family. It is always best when a child can maintain one consistent relationship by staying with the respite worker as needed. Call your local foster care agency and inquire about becoming a respite worker. Many states offer a stipend to offset the costs.

A FEW can go through the foster care certification training in your state. The entire training is free in most states, after which you can decide if you want to complete a home study and become a foster parent. The training is a prerequisite to the application process. This is a great learning and networking time with other foster families, and it will give you the information you need if you are considering becoming a foster parent or adopting through the foster system.

CHAPTER 7

A Change of Heart

Orphans and Racism

I often receive phone calls from couples considering adoption, but Steve's statement cut me to the core. "Johnny, if we adopt a black child, it will probably cut in half the number of churches that will allow me to minister in the South."

A Southern "transplant" like me, Steve pastored a church north of the Mason-Dixon line, but his heart was still in the South. Steve and his wife, Angela, were pursuing adoption, and they had just gotten a call from their local social services office with a possible match. Jake was six years old, healthy, and legally free for adoption. He was also African American.

Steve and Angela longed to move back to their hometown to raise their family, but he was concerned that the idea of a white family—particularly a pastor's family—with a black kid wouldn't go over well. I wanted to laugh and tell him it wasn't true. I wanted to say, "Racism is a thing of the past. It only happened back before the Civil Rights Movement and integration. I guess you really did sleep through American history class."

But the more I thought about it, I wasn't sure I could honestly say that. Would a predominantly white church hire a pastor with an African-American, Latino, or Asian child, or maybe even multiple children that didn't fit the typical "mold"? Would such a family be welcomed with open arms, or would they be ostracized and gossiped about by the community?

Does racism still exist in churches? It was a question I didn't want to face.

In 2011, members at an Eastern Kentucky church voted not to recognize interracial couples and families as members or let them take part in certain worship activities. The decision was made when a young woman in the community brought her fiancé, who was from Zimbabwe, to church. After the couple led a song together during a worship service, they were banned from future involvement. The church proposal stated that "parties of such [interracial] marriages will not be received as members, nor will they be used in worship services" or other church events, except for funerals.[1]

Similarly, in 2012, a Mississippi church refused to allow a wedding to take place on their property for one simple reason: The couple was African American. The wedding date had been set, the church property reserved, and the invitations mailed. Everything was approved and set to go, until a certain group of members "complained about the black couple having their wedding there." The day before their wedding, the couple received a phone call from the pastor, who informed them that the church was no longer available and offered to perform the wedding elsewhere.[2] In a predominantly white congregation, the idea of a black couple being married in their sanctuary was unthinkable.

Granted, these stories point to a few extreme cases; however, they suggest that some of our churches are still segregated. Racism lives on in many religious circles, even if in more subtle ways. Racial slurs and stereotypes are mentioned from the pulpit. Demeaning generalizations are made about visitors of different ethnic backgrounds. Off-color jokes are said about immigration laws and politics.

Tragically, racism does still exist in some churches. And this racism often prevents us from fully engaging with orphan care. When we respond with disdain and skepticism to "those poor black people" (or any other race), we disobey Scripture. As long as we hold on to racial prejudices and stereotypes, we will be incapable of having genuine compassion for the fatherless and responding in sacrificial obedience.

In Our DNA

Henry was the first black man I ever met. He talked differently than my family did, and his smile showed a few crooked teeth, but I rarely saw that smile. The deep lines on Henry's face and rough calluses on his hands spoke of hardships I could only dream of.

But I didn't notice or care. As a kid, I never really saw Henry as a person; he was just always "there" with my granddaddy. My granddaddy was a rough and tough policeman during the Civil Rights movement in Alabama, controlling mobs and locking up dissidents. When a stroke paralyzed the right side of his body, Henry became his constant caregiver. Henry bathed my grand-dad, changed his clothes, fed him, took him to the bathroom, and performed a host of other services.

Looking back now, it is kind of ironic that this white law enforcement officer was cared for by a black man. It was not exactly the most exciting job, but Henry never complained. Meanwhile, I just assumed that all black men did this kind of work.

I never remember having a real conversation with Henry. I never sat in the same room with him, relaxing, watching TV, or talking as friends. He was too "respectful" to associate with white folk. In my mind, as a ten-year-old kid, Henry was clearly "below" us. I will never forget the day we were watching an Alabama football game and discussing Walter Lewis. Lewis was the first black man to become a starting quarterback for the University of Alabama—a topic of hot debate among sports fans in the South. That's when I said it: "I wouldn't want a nigger quarterback. They definitely can't make decisions like a white guy can."

Just then, Henry walked around the corner and our eyes met. His face twisted up in deep pain, but only for an instant. Then it was gone. He shuffled across the room, head down, and dutifully helped granddaddy out of his recliner. They walked to the bathroom together—Henry's strong, dark arms supporting granddad's frail little body, his callused hands taking care of my grandpa in ways he couldn't care for himself.

I'm ashamed that my African-American son, JJ, will know that his dad called a person that name. But I did. I wonder how many of us are honest enough to admit we have held to racist thoughts and attitudes. Perhaps we have spoken or acted in ways that are blatantly racist as well.

Simply put, racism is the devaluing of another person. It's determining human value, intelligence, and worth based on skin color or culture, rather than the reality that each of us is made in God's image. Billy Graham wisely said,

> Racism is a sin precisely because it keeps us from obeying God's command to love our neighbor, and because it has its roots in pride and arrogance. Christians who harbor racism in their attitudes or actions are not following their Lord at this point, for Christ came to bring reconciliation—reconciliation between us and God, and reconciliation between each other.[3]

As much as we'd like to fancy twenty-first-century culture—and ourselves—as progressive, tolerant, and post-racial, it's just not true. That's because racial prejudice is part of our sin nature. It's in our DNA, so to speak, whether you're Caucasian, African American, Asian, Hispanic, or from any other ethnic group.

You don't have to *try* to be a racist. Think of it like an accent. Racism is as natural as my Southern Alabama drawl. Perhaps the reason we don't see our own bigotry is because it's so close to home. It's so deeply ingrained. Racism is just one expression of the self-righteousness deeply rooted in our hearts, apart from the redeeming grace of the gospel. I'm guessing you never took a "How to Be Racist" class, but you have likely had racist thoughts and attitudes. It's just part of our culture. It's part of who we are.

Unfortunately, the church is often one of the most segregated sectors of our society. If we took an honest look at most of our churches on any given Sunday, we would notice that segregation in the United States is at its peak in religious communities. There are a few glimmers of hope around the country. Most major cities now have at least one church that is truly multicultural in its staff and congregants. However, these churches are very few and far between.

For many of us, we don't even recognize our racism because we have never stepped outside of our "cultural cocoon." We have never tried to think differently. We have never challenged the norm.

We all see color. That is not a bad thing. Our claims to be "colorblind" when it comes to race ignore the reality of ethnic diversity. There is nothing wrong with racial and cultural differences; in fact, we should embrace diversity as evidence of the creativity and beauty of our Creator God. But we must be careful to avoid criticizing these differences, or viewing one race or ethnicity as better than another.

It's not our eyes that need to change. It's our hearts.

Confronting the Racist in Me

If racism is an issue of the heart, no amount of education or government reform will change our culture. This is not the kind of change that comes merely from human effort—from "trying harder" and "doing more." Confronting the racist in each one of us starts with a new understanding of the gospel that begins to transform our often-hard hearts. The true gospel of Jesus Christ frees us to see each person in a new way. As the apostle Paul put it, "In Christ there is not Greek and Jew, circumcision and uncircumcision, barbarian, Scythian, slave and free; but Christ is all and in all" (Col. 3:11). As we consider orphan care, this new understanding changes the way we see children and go about helping them.

I am afraid that many of us may participate in caring for orphans of different races out of guilt instead of grace. Maybe we see ourselves as helping "those poor kids in Africa or China," forgetting that each one is a unique and precious child formed in his or her mother's womb by God's hand, just as we were.

When we help orphans of another race or ethnicity just to boost our own ego, we miss the mark. Trying to earn God's favor or be recognized by others for our generosity turns the focus back on us and what we can do, rather than joining God in the work of healing and hope He longs to bring to these kids' lives out of His abundant grace. Even in their desperate need, each of these children is just as valuable to the Lord as you and I, yet often we can be tempted to see them as "less than." Blinded by prejudice, we cannot truly care for the fatherless and orphan as God commands us to. We need a heart shift in order to grasp that not one of us is better or more deserving than any other person on this earth—regardless of skin color, socioeconomic level, or culture.

In my own life, I've been convicted of my haughty, selfish attitude when it comes to orphan care. I want to serve God on *my* terms. I want to pick and choose the type of orphans my family will minister to and the type of kids we'll adopt. I want what's comfortable, easy, and makes sense. Even without my own racist attitudes, I realize that being a father to a child of another race means I have to deal with other people's racist tendencies, and it is sometimes very difficult. But I cannot let other people's sinful words and actions keep me from caring for orphans of every race and ethnic background in the way God wants me to.

I'll never forget the first day we met JJ. Sitting in a Dairy Queen booth across from his foster mom, I was forced to ask myself some hard questions. Here I was with a little black boy in my arms. It brought back a lot of memories of Henry and other times in my life that I had judged people based on their skin color.

But I also thought about my high school friends. Dexter, Gilbert, David, and Eric were the first African Americans that I really saw as people. They were my classmates, my teammates, and my friends. Saks High School was predominantly white, with the exception of one bus from Central City. Every kid on that bus was African American, including Dexter and the other guys. On the days we had football games, they'd come over to my house after school and hang out until game time. My mother tells me it caused quite a stir in our neighborhood when people saw black and white kids playing in the street together.

Holding JJ that day at Dairy Queen, I knew that I had to be honest with myself. *Have I truly repented of my racist past? Are Beth and I really prepared to raise a black child?* I had to count the cost for him and for us.

When my family walks into a restaurant or the grocery store or the movie theater, we often get the same reaction. People stare. Some look in admiration, some in disgust, and some don't know what to make of it. You'd think from their faces that we're the craziest people on the earth. I guess having five kids of three different ethnicities isn't exactly "normal."

In the process of JJ's adoption, I also had to ask myself how our church would respond. What type of diversity existed in my church? How would we be accepted with an African-American son? Were we willing to change churches if needed? Would there be spiritual African-American men and women in my church for my child to see as role models on a weekly basis?

When Caucasian people adopt Asian or European children, it's almost viewed as a "cool" thing to do. However, adopting an African-American child is sometimes not as accepted. The looks that we get from both white and black people are very interesting. Many people think we are cute with our Asian kids, but we are often looked down on because of our African-American child.

I had someone ask me recently, "Do you think he'll ever wonder why his parents are white and he is black?" They asked as if this were reason enough not to adopt a child of a different race. Of course he will wonder. It is blatantly obvious that three of my children are adopted. Each will have friends that asks questions. It's all part of the deal.

Lonnie Wesley is one of my best friends. Lonnie pastors an African-American church in Pensacola, and we have had countless gut-honest conversations about race. He and his wife, Latonya, were our biggest supporters in JJ's adoption.

Lonnie called me one day, and his voice was troubled. "Johnny, there's a black woman in our church who adopted a biracial child a few years back. To see this little girl you would think that she's a black kid. This lady just got a call today about a newborn biological sibling who is being placed for adoption. The problem is that this time, both parents are white."

I thought back to our decision to adopt JJ. We didn't call Lonnie and get his opinion. We didn't call any of our African-American friends and ask if they would be "OK" with it. But a black person adopting a white child was groundbreaking in Pensacola. My response to Lonnie was, "Is she prepared to be Rosa Parks and sit in the front of the bus?"

While this woman wasn't physically risking her life like Rosa Parks did, she would certainly be challenging cultural norms and taking a risk by adopting a white child. She would be the first in her community to have the courage to do so. This woman has every right to adopt a Caucasian baby and keep the siblings together. I applaud her for her courage. But she—and we—need to realize the ridicule, criticism, and questions that we will face if we have a biracial family. And perhaps we also need to examine our own hearts to see if we have been the ones ridiculing, criticizing, and questioning.

When the kids at school poke fun at your son or daughter because "your mommy and daddy look different," what will you say? When that crazy uncle tells a racist joke over Christmas dinner, how will you respond? Will you count the costs? Are you willing to stand up and speak up to anyone who might infringe upon the dignity of your child—even if it means losing some of your closest relationships?

I pray that you will never be faced with these kinds of situations. I pray your family and friends will support your cross-cultural adoption and see your child the way Jesus does.

Rethinking the Good Samaritan

Search "Good Samaritan stories" on Google and you'll get about 2.28 million results in 0.07 seconds. There are countless stories of random acts of kindness and selfless giving to people in need. The parable of the Good Samaritan ranks right up there with Noah's Ark, Adam and Eve, and baby Jesus as the most well-known Bible stories. Most Americans know what a "Good Samaritan" is. It has become a cultural reference to identify anyone who helps a person in need without any expectation in return. A Good Samaritan may rescue a child from a burning building, perform CPR at the site of a car wreck, or tow a drowning vacationer to shore.

But as I look at the parable Jesus told in Luke 10, I'm afraid we have missed a very important part of this story. You see, the parable of the good Samaritan isn't just a lesson in "being kind." Through this story, Jesus confronts racism. Did you ever notice that the Samaritan doesn't have a name? Jesus simply refers to him as "a Samaritan." He's a nobody who just happens to represent an entire race of people—a people viewed as illegitimate, biracial, second-class citizens.

Racism runs deep, all the way back to biblical times. When the northern kingdom of Israel was destroyed in 722 BC, foreigners colonized the land. Scripture describes it: "Then the king of Assyria brought people from Babylon, Cuthah, Avva, Hamath, and Sepharvaim and settled them in place of the Israelites in the cities of Samaria" (2 Kings 17:24). Over time, the local Jews intermarried with these foreigners, leading to the development of a unique ethno-religious people commonly known as "Samaritans." The full-blooded Jews weren't exactly friends with the Samaritans. Because of their mixed blood, Samaritans were ostracized, looked down on, and treated with hostility.

Jewish-Samaritan interactions were few and far between and were rarely cordial. In fact, Jewish travelers would even go out of their way to avoid Samaritan towns. At best, these two racial groups tolerated each other. At worst, they killed each other. So when the religious leaders accused Jesus of being possessed by a demon and being a Samaritan, their racism was blatant (see John 8). When Jesus spoke to the Samaritan woman at the well, she was clearly shocked because "Jews do not associate with Samaritans" (John 4:9). Racism is not just a modern-day problem.

The Jews hated the Samaritans, and vice versa. Despite this cultural chasm, the Samaritan placed the injured man on his own donkey, took him to an inn, and paid for whatever the man needed. If the story had happened today, the Samaritan would have put the man in his car, headed to the hospital, pulled out his credit card, and told the receptionist, "Charge it all to me, no matter what the cost." I imagine the process wasn't fun or exciting for the Samaritan. It was messy, draining, and hard. It required energy, sacrifice, and commitment in order to bring hope to the injured man.

It's no coincidence that Jesus chose a Samaritan as the hero of His story. It's like He was saying, "If you want to enter My kingdom, become like the one you're racist toward. Reach out in love to help those who you ostracize, those you look down on, those you despise."

His command is radical: Love your neighbor. "And who is my neighbor?" The religious leader—and we, too—look for a loophole (see Luke 10:25–29). But if we're honest with ourselves, there's no way around it. Loving our neighbor includes loving orphaned and vulnerable children, no matter their skin color or religious background. After all, Jesus died for all of us—Jew and Gentile, black and white.

Changing Our Hearts, Changing Our Culture

Stereotypes die hard. As I write this chapter, I'm sitting in a local coffee shop late at night. When I walked in and scanned the room, I was faced with a tough decision. There were only two empty tables. One table was right next to several rough-looking white guys who were covered with tattoos and piercings. They were not really my type. The other free spot was beside a couple of innocent-looking teenage girls playing a board game. I sat beside the girls.

It was a bad choice. I had to put my earbuds in to drown out their filthy language. When the girls went outside to take a smoke, I breathed a sigh of relief, but not for long. They brought the smoke back in with them. When the rough-looking guys got up to leave, I was surprised to see one of them stick a Bible in his bag—a bag that had my church's name on it. They had just finished their Bible study. Often, our stereotypes and assumptions are just plain wrong. They can keep us from seeing people the way Jesus does.

So how do we get rid of these stereotypes and assumptions and start to interact with the "Samaritans" in our lives? We must begin with love and friendship. Jesus said that we should love our neighbor as we love ourselves (Mark 12:31). That's hard. But we need to develop friendships with people who don't look like us, dress like us, or talk like us. Think about your circle of friends. If they're all just like you, how are you developing Christlikeness and loving your neighbor?

After a recent school talent show, I looked on with curiosity as my son James interacted with his new friend Travis. Let me tell you, a short Chinese deaf boy and a tall African-American hearing kid are an unlikely match, but as I watched the boys hanging out together, I found something incredibly beautiful and humbling. Even when we first walked into the school gym and James saw Travis, his face lit up. He didn't see a black person; he saw his friend. When Travis ran up to James and began signing to him, he wasn't doing it out of pity. Travis genuinely enjoyed trying to communicate with James.

I noticed Travis's dad and made a point to introduce myself and strike up a conversation. As we stood and watched our kids try to communicate, I couldn't help but think to myself, *This is where racial reconciliation starts.* Maybe it means walking across the room, across the fellowship hall, across the street, or across the basketball court. But I challenge you, just as my son challenged me, to do something.

If Jesus is building His church from "every tribe and language and people and nation" (Rev. 5:9), shouldn't we do the same? We, as Christ followers, must be willing to cross racial lines and break down cultural barriers to help orphaned and vulnerable children in our own country and around the world.

If we are serious about following Christ to care for orphaned and vulnerable children, we have to deal directly with the issue of racism in our hearts and our churches. We must confront racism wherever it exists, repent where repentance is needed, and make appropriate changes.

Acts 1:8 offers a tangible model for cultural influence and change—"you will be My witnesses in Jerusalem, Judea and Somaria, and to the ends of the earth." We must ask ourselves how we can confront racism in our "Jerusalem" and begin to live in such a way that we become culture-changers. Often, we focus on "the ends of the earth" while neglecting what's close to home. But racial reconciliation is needed in every area of the world, starting with your own church and community. Supporting and encouraging families to adopt children from other races here in the U.S. is one huge step in welcoming orphans of every tribe, language, people, and nation into your local church body.

A simple way for churches to create change is through partnering with churches of different cultures. Encourage your church
leaders to take proactive steps to build friendships and interact with
local bodies of believers of different ethnic backgrounds. If your
church is predominantly Caucasian, reach out to Korean churches,
Hispanic churches, and African-American churches. Step outside of
your "cultural cocoon." This does not mean having the local black
teenage choir sing a gospel number in your Christmas pageant. Real
partnership means doing ministry together, worshipping together,
taking mission trips together, and sharing small groups together.

I want my black son to have black men and women in his life
who are spiritual leaders and hold positions of authority. I believe
that this is critical to his growth and nurture. If we, as a family,
only hang out with white people, what will JJ gather about how I
really feel toward African Americans? What will James and Xiaoli
think about how I really view Chinese people?

If we are going to encourage adoption and orphan care without
racial boundaries, we have to begin thinking about the cultures we
are creating and perpetuating in our churches, our workplaces, and
our homes. Racial reconciliation involves far more than just putting
people of different skin colors in the same room. It includes cultivat-
ing and celebrating a church and family culture of diversity.

Confessions of a Recovering Racist

I was a Southern boy who loved Jesus and looked down on
African Americans. Now, because of God opening my eyes to this
new aspect of the gospel, I am a recovering racist who is passionate
about confronting prejudice and building friendships that bridge
that gap. I thank God for men like Dexter Tolbert (my friend from
high school), Lonnie Wesley, Elijah Hicks (JJ's foster dad), and
Leo Day (my running partner). Each of these men plays a huge

role in my life as mentors and friends, and each of them is African American. They have laughed with me, shaken their heads at me, confronted me, and prayed with me. In trying to be a good dad to JJ, I have asked many ignorant questions about afros, skin care, and "black culture," but these men have loved me unconditionally. They have shown me grace, not judgment.

The gospel makes it possible for us to change and to see people as Jesus does, but it takes humility and commitment. We must be willing to invest in relationships, have gut-honest conversations, listen carefully, seek to understand, and love our neighbors. This is how we fight racism—not with guns, posters, or just politics. We must be contemplative about our past, honest about our present, and intentional about our future.

One of the greatest moments of my life came in July 2010. I was asked to preach at Pastor Lonnie's church, which is an African-American congregation. As I stood and looked out at the crowd, I lost it. Tears streamed down my face as I thought about their unjust history and my racist past. *What a strange irony*, I thought, *that a former bigot like me has the privilege of speaking to my brothers and sisters who I once viewed as "less human."*

If you are a follower of Jesus Christ, racism is an issue you can't afford to dismiss. Racism keeps us from practicing pure religion. It's not only the government, pop culture, or gangs that need to change—it's me and you. Confronting the racism in our own hearts is the first step to truly loving our neighbor and accepting orphans who don't look or act just like us.

What You Can Do

ANYONE can evaluate your current relationships to determine just how diverse your friendships are. When was the last time you had someone from a different race over to your home? When was the last time you invited someone of a different ethnicity to your church? Make it a goal to build intentional friendships with people of a different race or culture in the next year. Challenge your own discriminatory tendencies by spending time with and sharing life with people of different cultures and ethnic backgrounds. Step outside your own culture and educate yourself. Look for families in your congregation who have adopted cross-culturally, and give them encouraging words of affirmation. If you hear or see racism of any kind in your church, confront it and do not excuse it.

MANY can truly engage your church leaders in a conversation about intentionally breaking down racial and cultural barriers by partnering with churches of diverse racial backgrounds. Suggest combining worship services, mission trips, and small groups at various times throughout the year. It is also critical to be intentional with your youth and children's events. A suburban church and an inner-city church can come together and host two weeks of VBS during the summer—one in the suburbs and one in the inner city. For families adopting interracially, this will provide an environment for these children that strengthens their worldview. You can also become involved in mentoring children of a different ethnic background who are in foster care or at-risk children in your community.

A FEW can prayerfully consider adopting a child of a different race. By doing so, you will make a bold statement about your stance against racism. There are definite challenges in raising a child of another culture, but the child is well worth the risk. Seek God together as a couple about what He is calling you to as a family.

CHAPTER 8

More Than Sandwich Boards

Orphans and Abortion

Jake was born with severe medical issues. The doctors told his birth mother he would live for a few months, at most. As a young single mom, she wasn't able to provide the special care he needed, so she asked a nurse to call an adoption agency to see if they could find a home for her precious little Jake. Lauren and Gary welcomed baby Jake into their family for a temporary placement, but the agency did not pursue an adoption plan for him because of the doctors' prognosis. This little boy was destined to die without a family.

However, as Lauren and Gary began to pray over Jake and the weeks passed by, they felt the Lord was beginning to stir something in their hearts. They called their caseworker one morning and said, "We want to officially adopt Jake, and we need to hurry since we know he doesn't have very long left in this world."

The caseworker was, understandably, very surprised. She asked the couple if they were aware of the significant costs involved. She also explained that Jake would likely not live long enough for the adoption to even be completed. Lauren and Gary were well aware of these challenges, but this only fueled their sense of urgency. Their decision was unwavering, and they responded, "Jake needs a mom and a dad, no matter how short his life on earth might be."

Three years later, Jake is still alive. While severely handicapped, he has a mother and a father. In his short life, he has experienced the love of a family.

Jake will not die an orphan.

But for many other children like Jake, the story ends quite differently. Birth defects and other special needs lead many women to consider abortion. According to one study, "an estimated 92 percent of all women who receive a prenatal diagnosis of Down syndrome choose to terminate their pregnancies."[1] That means only eight babies out of every one hundred who have Down syndrome will have a chance at life. Our culture's view of abortion has caused many to devalue life. It's a quick fix that eliminates children with an illness or disability before they're even born.

Much of the Christian response to abortion has been political, with the hope of reversing abortion laws to save the lives of innocent children. But what if *Roe v. Wade* is overturned? What then? Have we fulfilled our Christian duty to stand for life and "speak up for those who have no voice" (Prov. 31:8)? Without a doubt, you and I would rejoice about saving the lives of these innocent children, but many of us would likely stop there.

What about the ninety-two out of every one hundred babies with Down syndrome who would actually be born into this world? *Many of these special needs children will need a family.* Many parents, like Jake's birth mother, would be ill equipped to care for these children with special needs. As one mother who aborted her baby with Down syndrome reflected, "I don't know if I was a strong enough person to raise a child like that."[2]

If *Roe v. Wade* is ever overturned, the foster care system will likely be flooded with special needs cases. Will we, as God's people, be prepared to take care of the children who were not aborted, but then abandoned? If we claim to be "pro-life," we must be willing to take an honest look at our attitudes toward children with disabilities. We must be honest with ourselves about how the church has handled and in some cases even mishandled this issue.

Since the *Roe v. Wade* court decision on January 22, 1973, the evangelical reaction has often been viewed by the world as one of violence, judgment, and political activism. Our history isn't one I'm particularly proud of. But to take a frank look at abortion, we must stop pointing the finger at the "baby killers" and be willing to consider where the church—or those who claim to represent the church—has been misguided, ineffective, or just plain wrong.

Kill the Killers?!

"It's not a fetus; it's a baby!" "Abortion isn't healthcare because killing isn't healing!" "Planned Parenthood lies to you!" "Stop the baby slashers!"

When driving down Ninth Avenue in Pensacola, Florida, you will pass my kids' former elementary school, Krispy Kreme Donuts, Sacred Heart Hospital . . . and American Family Planning.[3] Protestors have been known to line the sidewalk outside the clinic, sometimes displaying grotesque pictures of aborted babies. These well-meaning activists sometimes even raise their voices at the women walking through the parking lot to the Planned Parenthood office, "Abortion is murder! Save your baby's life or face God's judgment!"

Every time I passed by and saw the protestors lined up, I felt uncomfortable. I wrestled internally. Honestly, I am not sure how effective their approach was, because I know it doesn't usually go too well when people scream in *my* face. Yet among conservative Christians who feel deeply about abortion, we often struggle to know what to do to take a stand for life.

Looking in, the pro-choice world pegs most concerned Christians as extremists. Violence toward abortionists and clinics is assumed to be accepted and possibly even encouraged by the Christian community. Pensacola is no stranger to such events. American Family Planning of Pensacola first made the news in 1984 in what is known as the Christmas Day Bombings. Matthew Goldsby and James Simmons bombed three Pensacola abortion clinics as a "gift to Jesus on his birthday."[4] Goldsby and Simmons went on to serve ten years in prison.

This was just the beginning of the "Holy War," as *People* magazine dubbed it. On March 10, 1993, Michael Griffin shot and killed Dr. David Gunn, who was entering another clinic across town. The violence continued on July 29, 1994, back at the clinic on Ninth Avenue, then known as The Ladies Center. Paul Hill gunned down Dr. John Britton and his security escort, James Barrett. Hill would become the first person executed for killing an abortion doctor. On January 1, 2012, Bobby Joe Rogers fire-bombed the Pensacola building, resulting in $300,000 of damage. For whatever reason, Griffin, Hill, and other extremists believed that God wanted them to bring judgment on the leaders of the abortion movement. And they used Scripture to try and justify their actions.

As a Pensacola local, I was faced with daily reminders of all the wrong that has been carried out by extremists in the name of being "pro-life." But God also gave me a reminder of how Christians can tangibly show love to the people associated with an abortion clinic. As I would drive by the Family Planning building, I often noticed a grandmotherly woman standing in the small grass strip out front. She had no sign, and she did not chant.

She would pray. This lady prayed for the women who were scheduled to have an abortion that day. She prayed for their children. She prayed for the doctors, nurses, and office staff. If a young woman would take it, she would hand them a small pamphlet that read, "You still have options, and adoption is one of them."

This woman's simple faith challenged my pride and harsh judgment of the "Christian" response to abortion. Some of us yell and scream and hold up signs for a few hours. Others make a point to vote for pro-life candidates. But there are still others, like this woman, who genuinely desire to reach out in love and offer hope to those who are considering or have had an abortion. I pray more of us will be like her.

Creating a culture of life encompasses much more than just protesting murder. It must fundamentally begin with our hearts, and we have much to learn from this Pensacola woman who faithfully prays.

When It Hits Home

What happens when a Christian who pickets outside of an abortion clinic to show support for life discovers that a woman he or she knows and loves is faced with an unplanned pregnancy? What is the biblical way—the pro-life way—to respond to that woman's situation?

She's the scared high schooler. Her parents are leaders in the church, and they can't stand the thought of public disgrace. She's the student leader in the youth group who just started dating the youth pastor's son and went too far. She's the college student who thought she was in love but came to a rude awakening when the man of her dreams walked out on her. She's the pre-K Sunday school teacher who thought if she had sex with her boyfriend, he'd marry her and they could settle down and have a family. She's the young mom with three kids already whose husband pressures her to get an abortion because he says they won't have enough money to provide for yet another child. She's the divorced woman in a rebound relationship trying to numb the pain of abandonment. She's the forty-year-old in a midlife crisis who is worried about the risk of giving birth to a baby with Down syndrome.

Maybe she's your friend, your sister, or your daughter.

When that woman looks down at the pregnancy test, her heart fills with panic. She feels alone, afraid, and overwhelmed. She is desperately searching for answers and support. In many cases, tragically, she finds none. Kim Conroy, Focus on the Family's Sanctity of Human Life Director, points out that "many women choose abortion out of fear or a perceived lack of support."[5]

In my own research gathered from talking with pregnancy resource center directors, I was shocked at what I discovered. I asked the center directors, "Of the single, expectant mothers that you meet and talk with who claim to be Christians, how many would you say feel supported and cared for by their church?"

Their response: Only one or two out of every ten. That means eight or nine out of every ten churchgoing single, expectant women feel alienated, judged, or misunderstood. The numbers speak for themselves: *When these women need the church most, we often turn our backs.*

A recent study confirms that "social reasons" are actually the biggest influence in leading women to abort a child:[6]

Social Reasons (given as primary reason)	
—Feels unready for child/responsibility	25%
—Feels she can't afford baby	23%
—Has all the children she wants / other family responsibilities	19%
—Relationship problem / single motherhood	8%
—Feels she isn't mature enough	7%
—Interference with education or career plans	4%
—Parents or partner wants abortion	<1%

Personally, this is an issue that really hits home for Beth and me. Not long after Heather (our first child) was born, we went out on a date night. The waitress serving us was young, pregnant, and appeared to be unmarried. I don't remember exactly what crass comment I made about the girl after she walked away from our table, but I knew that I had hurt Beth deeply from the look on her face.

Not long after we started dating, Beth had shared with me one of her most painful experiences. At the age of seventeen, she discovered that she was pregnant. Her parents had given her two choices: Drop out of school and become a single mom or have an abortion. Adoption was not given as an option.

Beth believed that if she chose to parent, she would be ostracized, judged, and maybe even kicked out of her youth group. She thought that she would be alone and that no man would ever consider marrying her if she already had a child. As a result, she chose abortion.

That night on our date, as I stood in judgment over our waitress, Beth looked across the table at me and said, "You know, that was your wife just a few years ago. At least she is giving her baby a chance at life." Sometimes the truth hurts.

I have had the privilege of walking this journey with Beth. I believe that she is the most courageous woman I have ever met, and I have learned so much from her since that conversation. I have watched God bring emotional, psychological, and spiritual healing in her life over the years.

However, it is still difficult at times. A well-meaning Christian friend makes a comment like, "I just can't believe anyone could kill their own child," never imagining the impact of her words on women like Beth. A pastor gets up on Sanctity of Life Sunday and begins to talk about the evils of abortion. Instead of preaching a sermon filled with grace and truth, the pastor is more concerned about getting that "one-liner" to bring the crowd to a rousing "amen" or even a standing ovation like a political rally. Meanwhile, Beth, and others like her, fight back the tears.

Reflecting on these experiences, Beth recently wrote,

> My mind drifts back to those very confusing days as a seventeen-year-old—wanting to do the right thing, but feeling like I didn't have any options. I also think about the many children who were born but are languishing in an orphanage or the foster care system. I have traveled the world and seen some of the poorest children on the planet. My heart breaks for each of those children who desperately need families, while the church applauds a political stance. They have no clue.
>
> I am thankful for the grace that God has given and made evident in my life. But, it's hard not to play the "what if" game and consider how things would have been different if my parents

> and the church had been supportive of adoption.
> I know I cannot go back and change the past, and
> I know God's righteousness covers my sin. But I
> can't say enough about how important the role of
> the church is in helping women choose life.

The evangelical church, in majority with the Catholic church, has made a statement in the United States (and in most countries around the world) that abortion is not an acceptable solution to unplanned pregnancy. We preach—and rightly so—on the sanctity of life and the evils of abortion. But one night and one bad decision later, a woman in our congregation discovers that she is now in the middle of one of the most important decisions of her life.

Then what? If we say we are pro-life, we must begin by truly loving and caring for every woman who is pregnant, no matter what her marital status might be. We must also commit to loving and caring for her child, regardless of any physical or psychological challenges that child may face. This requires humility and a change of perspective.

Abortion isn't just "out there" in the secular world. It's a decision that many women in our churches wrestle with. Statistics estimate that nearly 40 percent of American women have had an abortion.[7] Studies show that one in five abortion patients identify themselves as born-again, evangelical, charismatic, or fundamentalist. Overall, nearly 75 percent of women obtaining an abortion report a religious affiliation of some kind.[8] Let's be honest—being a Christian doesn't exempt us from temptation, doesn't remove our sex drives, and doesn't make us immune to poor choices.

How easy it is to judge and to assume that all women who have abortions are promiscuous and use abortion as birth control to avoid the consequences. Too often, we treat women with unplanned pregnancies like they are harlots, rather than real people with deep heart needs. I have seen this tragic reality far too often when a young woman gets pregnant.

The church often doesn't know what to do when an unmarried woman gets pregnant. Do we tolerate sexual sin by throwing a baby shower and treating a single mom the same as the young couple who were virgins when they got married? Or do we punish girls who get pregnant out of wedlock to "set an example" to the rest of the congregation?

Most Christians don't want to be seen as glorifying sex outside of marriage; so, many times, we do nothing for the mother-to-be. At best she feels a lack of support, but in many cases, she is ostracized and gossiped about, and perhaps she is even asked to leave the church before she starts to "show." While a pregnant girl is often demonized, little is said about the father of the child, and we all know it takes two to tango. We call the girl terrible names, but the guy gets off scot-free just because he doesn't have a growing belly.

And here's the strange irony. If the mother-to-be does make the courageous choice to protect the life within her—a choice Christians say is the right choice—she is then often left to fend for herself. We hush up this girl's shameful secret, abandoning her at the time when she desperately needs love, support, and wisdom the most.

As conservatives, we proudly turn our backs so we can't be accused of condoning sin. But our silence condemns us; doing nothing is a sin when a life is on the line. We are passive bystanders to the murder of innocent children. In many cases, we encourage it—either by our words or our lack of support. The problem is not just the abortionists; it's us. Too often, the Planned Parenthood counselor is the only person in a girl's life who seems to care. This is a tragedy.

I firmly believe that God's Word says premarital sex is sin. I'm not saying we should tolerate sin in the name of love. Wisdom is needed to navigate this challenge, particularly in today's sex-crazed culture. The *New York Times* recently reported a shocking cultural trend: "A child out of wedlock is the new normal . . . more than half of births to American women under 30 occur outside marriage."[9] We must educate our young people about the sanctity of marriage and the importance of purity. But, living in a sinful world, we will always have to face the reality of mistakes.

While there's no easy answer here, the church's dismissal of a single mother's needs is a far cry from Jesus' response to the adulteress: "Neither do I condemn you. . . . Go, and from now on do not sin anymore" (John 8:11). He stood up for her; we gang up against her. He lovingly admonished her; we condemn her. He extended grace; we give her a cold shoulder.

Among Christ followers, I think repentance plays a huge part in how Jesus would have us respond to unplanned pregnancies. Too often, we judge a girl's growing stomach, but fail to consider the attitude of her heart. When a woman has a repentant spirit, there are definitely appropriate ways to show our support for her and her family. She should in no way feel ostracized by the body of Christ. On the contrary, the church should be on the front lines of encouraging and empowering this mother-to-be to choose life for her baby. Whether she chooses motherhood or adoption, we must honor the brave decision she is making and support her emotionally, financially, and spiritually.

I have often heard the argument that if a church helps such young women, it will communicate that we don't take sin seriously and will encourage all the young people to go out and have sex. What a poor excuse and an easy "out." The stakes are high—it's about life or death for the baby. If the love and grace shown to a pregnant teenager in your church influences another girl in the church to get pregnant, she likely has much bigger issues that need to be dealt with. We dare not withhold grace, love, and support from one mother-to-be for fear of encouraging another girl to engage in sexual behavior.

I do realize that not all Christians cast aside pregnant single mothers. Many churches and nonprofit organizations have started homes that take in pregnant women, cover their expenses, counsel the women about life-giving options such as adoption, and give them a place to live during their pregnancies. Many women, couples, and families minister in similar ways, opening up their homes to women facing unexpected pregnancies. However, in conservative circles, this is often the exception, rather than the norm.

Am I Really Pro-Life?

I always thought that I was pro-life. But as God began to soften my heart toward orphan care and adoption, I began to realize that I really wasn't pro-life at all. I was actually just anti-abortion. I said all of the right things about life beginning at conception and abortion being murder, but never once did I do anything to act in a pro-life way. It was just words—a theological belief and a political stance, but not a lifestyle.

I began to think back to the sermons I had heard (and preached) on Sanctity of Human Life Sunday. Every sermon was little more than a treatise on how God hates murder and murderers. We should have honestly called it Sanctity of Pre-born Human Life Sunday. But there is so much more at stake.

I firmly believe that the abortion culture has devalued life. As an ordained Southern Baptist minister, I agree and stand by the official statement of the Convention, which reads: "Procreation is a gift from God, a precious trust reserved for marriage. At the moment of conception, a new being enters the universe, a human being, a being created in God's image. This human being deserves our protection, whatever the circumstances of conception."[10]

Barney Frank, one of the most liberal representatives to have served in the U.S. Congress, made an interesting observation about conservatives. This statement was in response to the movement of the Moral Majority in the early 1980s: "The Moral Majority supports legislators who oppose abortions but also oppose child nutrition and day care. From their perspective, life begins at conception and ends at birth."[11]

Congressman Frank made a valid point. It takes humility to actually listen to and consider this indictment from someone that I disagree with on almost every political issue. But think about it: We fight and fight for the unborn but do relatively little for children who are dying every day from lack of clean water, food, or proper shelter. Can we really claim to be pro-life if we fail to consider the importance of caring for any and all at-risk children? We might more accurately be called "pro-birth."

Standing for the sanctity of life involves so much more than wearing a sandwich board and protesting in front of an abortion clinic. Christians often have little to no credibility on the subject of abortion because Barney Frank hit us right between the eyes. Our claims and our actions don't match up. With some exceptions, we call ourselves "pro-life," but our lifestyles, our priorities, and our budgets often show that we are little more than "anti-abortion." And the world sees it.

As long as there are more than 100,000 children in the U.S. foster system who are waiting to be adopted, I don't think we will ever be taken seriously. So let's turn that around. If we really want to make a statement about children and how much we believe in the sanctity of life, let's start a campaign to get every adoptable child in the foster care system into a loving home in the next twelve months. That would speak far louder than any tract, any sandwich board, or any march in Washington, D.C.

We desperately need more families adopting hard-to-place children. Many children awaiting adoption are of mixed races. Many are not infants. Many face special needs because of their mother's unhealthy lifestyle, poor nutrition during pregnancy, or genetic predisposition. Their mothers chose life, but now they need families to provide a loving home and future for their children.

Our son JJ is one of these children. This precious little boy was in the NICU the first nine months of his life because of severe health complications. When his birth mother took him home, he soon suffered from failure to thrive. To this young woman's credit, she did try to parent him. She didn't have an abortion, and she truly loved her son. But as a young girl in the foster system, she was totally unable to provide for his medical needs. Hoping for a better future for her son than she could provide, this courageous mom relinquished him to the state.

As a result, we got a call from a caseworker at our local foster care agency. "I know your family has adopted several deaf children," she said. "Would you be open to one more, or do you know of anyone interested in adopting a deaf child? I have a little boy named JJ that we're trying to place. He was born at twenty-five weeks gestation and is a miracle baby. He is on a feeding tube for all solids and liquids. He has chronic lung disease and cerebral palsy . . ."

As she went on, I thought to myself, *Definitely not an option.*

"He is deaf and blind," she continued. "But he is a precious little baby. Honestly, he shouldn't even be alive, but he's a fighter."

Trying not to sound heartless, I responded, "Thank you so much for considering our family, but I think that is too many disabilities for us to handle at this point. I travel a lot with my work,

Beth works full time, and we already have four children—two of them with special needs."

I hung up the phone and honestly didn't give JJ another thought until three weeks later, when I received a follow-up e-mail with the subject line "Anyone?" The social worker wondered if I had come across any families interested in adopting this special little boy. She also attached a picture.

My heart skipped a beat as I stared into the eyes of an adorable African-American toddler. He had a huge smile on his face as he sat at a table putting a puzzle together. I was shocked. I had imagined a shriveled, incapacitated child lying there helplessly, hooked up to a bunch of tubes. I e-mailed the caseworker back immediately. The message was something along the lines of, "Uhhh, I think you must have mixed up the pictures. There's no way this little boy could be the same child you described to me on the phone. He looks so, well, normal."

Within a half hour, I received a reply. The social worker explained that some of her initial information was not accurate. JJ was deaf but not blind. He did have cerebral palsy, but only in his lower extremities, causing him to "toe walk." A G-tube feeding port was inserted in his stomach wall, but he was still completely mobile. Several times a day, his caregiver just needed to attach a tube to the port so he could receive food and water. JJ's lungs were the doctors' biggest concern. When he was born at twenty-five weeks, his lungs were undeveloped and barely functional, leading to nine months of specialized care in the NICU.

After praying together as a family, we cautiously began to move forward with adopting JJ. In May 2011, Elijah Jerrell Carr officially became a part of our family. This little boy really is a walking miracle. We recently met with a doctor specializing in neonatal care, and she was shocked to hear JJ's history.

"Children born at full term with his condition only have about a 50 percent chance of living." Her eyes teared up as she spoke. "I don't think I've ever heard of a child with his condition born at twenty-five weeks actually living."

We nearly missed out on the joy and blessing of JJ because we thought his case was "too hard." Even if his condition had been as bad as we initially thought, his life still would have been a blessing to us . . . because it is a *life* and we have the joy of helping him live it.

Is parenting a child with special needs hard work? Sure. Is it worth it? Without a doubt.

How many JJs will be born this week, this month, or this year? How many birth moms will choose to not have an abortion and then come to the realization that they cannot care for their child? How many women—even in your own church—will wrestle between the "quick fix" of an abortion and the "long haul" of choosing life for their child?

Who will be there for moms in crisis? Who will stand up on vulnerable children's behalf? Who will financially support couples in order to make adoption possible for kids with physical and psychological challenges? If God's people do not step in to offer hope and help, I fear for these children's futures. I fear for their lives. So should you.

Developing a Culture that Honors Life

Pro-life isn't just picketing or politics. It's valuing every single human life, both before and after birth. My friend Dean set a striking (and radical) example recently in his interaction with a Planned Parenthood leader. There were no guns and no bloodshed, but I can tell you, Dean's response made a lasting impact.

As a pastor who is passionate about life, Dean jumped at the invitation to speak on a panel about abortion and ethics at a major medical school. When he arrived at the event, he realized he would be speaking directly after the Planned Parenthood representative.

As the woman stood up to speak, Dean began to pray, "God, let me see this woman through your eyes." She spoke at length about how providing choices that ensure women's health requires courage and tenacity. She recalled to the audience the dirty names she had been called and how she had been ostracized and threatened. She shared how she had been forced to wear a bulletproof vest to work and how she often wondered if she would make it home alive.

As Dean took the mic, the crowd waited in suspenseful silence to hear how this conservative Christian would respond to the abortion supporter. "Ma'am, I am so sorry." Dean's words shocked everyone. Far from defensive or angry, he expressed genuine compassion. "On behalf of all evangelicals, I just want to take the opportunity to publicly apologize for the atrocities that have been committed in the name of saving lives. If Jesus were here, He would say the same thing."

Tears formed in the woman's eyes. It was likely the first time a Christian had ever seen her as a real person and not just "the enemy." It was the first time a conservative had spoken to her with respect and dignity, rather than calling her names or making angry threats. Dean went on to make a compelling case for the unborn and for life, but not by attacking or criticizing the opposition.

Jesus said in Luke 6:27, "Love your enemies, do what is good to those who hate you." That day, before a crowd of mostly pro-choice students, Dean didn't falter on his biblical stance about abortion. But he did more. He humbled himself. He admitted where the church, and those claiming to represent the church, have been wrong. He took responsibility that wasn't even his, and he was Jesus to this woman. He loved her.

We need more Deans among us.

We must speak up against the lie that violence or derogatory behavior toward abortionists and post-abortive women is justified or biblical. Nothing could be further from the truth. Some of us need to confront friends and those in our circle of influence who are misguided in their response to abortion, and all of us need to examine our own hearts to see where we've been wrong. Given the opportunity to speak about abortion in public settings, we must embody Dean's humble and gentle spirit. We must take the high road and offer apologies for those who have used the name of Jesus wrongly to commit violence.

Also, when we speak up against abortion but fail to also actively encourage adoption, foster care, and supporting children in poverty, we present a one-sided view of the issue. In our pursuit of stopping the abortion movement, we have often lost the bigger picture of building a culture of life. Mike Huckabee put it well when he said:

> In today's debates, the issue is often obscured
> by the debate about abortion, which centers on
> the right of a pregnant woman to choose the dis-
> position of her unborn child without any interfer-
> ence or input from the father, the family, or the
> federal government. But the culture of life is so
> much more.[12]
>
> I'm not anti-abortion, I'm pro-life, and there's
> a fundamental difference. I'm not against some-
> thing. I'm for something. I'm for the idea that
> your life and every other life has equal value,

and every life should be treated with dignity and
respect and honor.[13]

What are we doing for the babies who are being born into
the world? Is it enough that they have the chance to see the light
of day and breathe in oxygen? What about the children who are
starving every single day, dying of curable medical conditions, living in cramped and unsanitary orphanages, or stuck in the foster
care system waiting for a family?

Each child matters deeply to our God, but too often, not to
us. Maybe Congressman Frank was on to something: Many of
us have lived as if "life begins at conception and ends at birth."[14]
How shortsighted we've been. For every one verse in Scripture
about the evil of murder, there are at least ten or twenty verses
about taking care of the weak, needy, and vulnerable.

If we are going to speak against abortion—and we should—
we must also be the first to speak up for adoption. I challenge
you to the AA principle—Abortion and Adoption (not Alcoholics
Anonymous). Every time you talk to someone about abortion,
make sure you are also talking about adoption. For every anti-
abortion initiative or pro-life awareness event you organize, I
challenge you to also hold a meeting for potentially interested
foster parents.

Encourage your friends to consider adoption—and consider
it yourself. Talk about ways to help children in poverty. If we are
committed to fighting against abortion, we should be just as passionately fighting for adoption and orphan care to place vulnerable children in families both in the U.S. and around the world.

While special needs adoption is not for everyone, all of us can
get involved by financially supporting families who do feel God is
calling them to this. Adoption can be very expensive. How many
churches do you know that have an adoption fund to help families

with these expenses? Most churches see adoption as a personal, "optional" choice. But I challenge you to consider adoption differently. Many children who are waiting to be adopted (especially those with special needs) were likely born into the world after a difficult decision by their birth mother—a decision that we, the church, supported. So now we need to continue our pro-life stance by actually giving these children a loving family.

If we really value life, simply giving thirty dollars a month to a child-sponsorship program is not satisfactory. It's a starting point, but we must examine our hearts and ask God what it looks like to be pro-life and not just pro-birth.

Often, women choose abortion because they feel they have no other option. Christians and churches must be vocal about educating and encouraging women to consider the other options—motherhood and adoption.

If a woman chooses to keep her baby, we are called to support, encourage, and equip her as she learns how to parent. Being a single mom is tough financially, emotionally, and socially, particularly for teenagers. Mentoring, support groups, parenting skills classes, and help with childcare are all practical ways a church community can embrace a child and help a single mom overcome the challenges she faces.

If a woman places her baby for adoption, we are called to walk with her through this process and encourage her decision, rather than doubting or questioning it. She will need significant support, especially after her baby is placed with the adoptive family. With every story of adoption, there is a story of loss—both for the birth parents and for the child.

As already mentioned, sensitivity is very much needed in handling the issue of abortion within the church. If the statistics are true and 40 percent of American women have had an abortion, Beth is just one of many women in your church, neighborhood, and city who share a similar story. These women need companions in the journey of forgiveness and healing.

We will change our culture of abortion only as we develop a culture of life—as each one of us develops a sacrificial lifestyle that honors every human life, including children like Jake and JJ. As Christ followers, we should be first in line to adopt kids born with special needs or any other hard-to-place children. This is not a "government issue" to figure out. It is our call as the church to live out.

Currently, about 3 million women face unplanned pregnancies each year.[15] Of those, 1.2 million choose abortion[16] and only 18,000 choose adoption.[17] This is a tragedy.

As we elevate and support adoption—particularly special-needs adoption—we encourage abortion reduction and empower the body of Christ to care for all life, not just pre-born life.

It starts with you.

What You Can Do

ANYONE can financially support your local Christian pregnancy resource center. As you develop a relationship with the center, inquire about the number of referrals they are making for adoption and see if they feel adequately trained and comfortable in presenting adoption as an option. Offer to connect them with adoption agencies such as Bethany Christian Services for more information. You can also develop a support and discipleship group for women experiencing unplanned pregnancies in your church and community. Create an environment where other women can share their stories about previous abortions or decisions to place children for adoption.

MANY can volunteer at a pregnancy resource center to personally minister to women who are choosing life instead of abortion. You will want to talk to adoption specialists and seek out training so that you are fully educated on how to talk about adoption and parenting. Even if you aren't prepared or don't feel called to counsel personally, you can still volunteer at the center to help in other ways—whether by hosting fundraisers, organizing donations, providing childcare for events, or even offering to clean the premises on a regular basis.

A FEW can research and develop a plan to begin a special needs children's ministry in your church. Look at what others have done, develop some initial plans, and then prayerfully approach the church leadership about the possibility. This ministry is not just for adoptive families, as there are many families with special needs children. However, it will make a huge statement to families in your church who may consider fostering or adopting children with physical, emotional, or social challenges. Implementing a "Buddy System" (one adult assigned to one child) is one of the most practical and common ways of starting this ministry. This gives parents the opportunity to attend a worship service and know that their child is being cared for and loved.

CHAPTER 9

Buildings vs. Children
Orphans and the Church

That day back at James's orphanage in Zhenshi, China, really messed me up. Afterward, my dreams were filled with images of children wasting away—no families, very little food, tattered clothing, untreated medical issues, and few toys to play with. Every nightmare, the story was the same: A child was confined to a crude high chair with desperation in her eyes. She had a cleft lip and open palate, and she was starving to death. She was not just a statistic, but a real little girl who needed a family.

In every dream, I turned my back. I walked away from that shack of an orphanage and sat down behind my big oak desk as the Pastor of Ministry and Leadership Development. I was back where things were safe and comfortable—back to the American dream.

But that little girl's screams for help echoed through the corridors of my mind. Her eyes pierced to the core of my heart, shaking me out of my stupor. I spent many sleepless nights staring at our bedroom wall, trying to make sense of the blurred lines between dream world and reality. One night, as tears streamed down my face, I finally realized that my nightmare was real. This was the direction of my life. It was a puny, small, self-centered existence, but no one would have ever guessed. I was a pastor and a leader in my church and community.

I was still haunted by scenes of the orphanage as I sat in my plush office, crunching numbers for our next big project—a 10-million-dollar building initiative. The new building would include a large gymnasium, a fellowship hall, children's and pre-school suites, and a coffee shop.

As I looked over the building plans, something didn't match up. My mind flashed back to James's orphanage with its dirty and substandard conditions. I felt conflicted and confused. But what could I do about it? Those kids were on the other side of the world. I was called to take care of my own "flock" . . . right?

Are We Missing Something?

I sat in a strategy meeting with church leaders, bankers, architects, and contractors. Everyone else was excited, but my heart was not all there. *Ten million dollars,* I thought to myself. *One hundredth of that would be $100,000, which is more than enough to take care of the desperate conditions of every orphanage in Zhenshi.*

The bank made us an offer to finance the new building, but the economy was starting to falter in the recession of 2007. Our ability to get the loan became dependent on the success of our fundraising campaign. Timing was critical. After an hour of discussion, I turned to the banker and bluntly asked, "What is your drop-dead date for a commitment?"

In a last-ditch effort to shake my head free of Zhenshi and really take my job seriously, I told the committee, "If you give me a team, we'll make it happen." Nothing like commitment to bring my mind back to the present, right?

I really did try to do my best. We formed committees, wrote job descriptions, developed a plan, and even wrote a series of skits to go along with the sermons in the campaign. It was a noble cause, but I have to be honest with you, I was not all there.

One of the skits we wrote hit particularly close to home. A dad and his daughter were having a picnic lunch at the park. "We need to be generous, just like Jesus," the father said. "That's why your mom and I decided to give to the building campaign at church rather than going to the mountains on vacation this year." It was a perfect time for a teachable moment, only the daughter was not listening to her dad. She was watching a homeless man who sat on a nearby park bench. The daughter in the skit (played by my daughter, Heather) ended up walking over to the homeless guy and handing him her lunch. Dad was talking big about giving, but his little girl really "got" it. She lived it.

That girl was my daughter (literally and figuratively) . . . and the dad was me. In my heart, I felt very conflicted about giving any money to our building. I wanted to give it to my son's friends who were starving to death back in Zhenshi. These children were forgotten. They were dying of treatable health conditions, sitting in makeshift high chairs with flies buzzing around their excrement.

A few weeks after returning home from China, Beth and I learned that one of the infants at the orphanage—the one in my nightmares—had died of starvation because of her cleft lip and open palate. The cost of the surgery to save that child's life: $250. Trying to balance 10 million dollars, 250 dollars, and the value of one human life kept me up many nights. I have never experienced such a strong internal tug of war between competing priorities.

For growing churches, building a new building is one of the hardest decisions that leadership must wrestle through. Every pastor wants to be part of a growing church, and often, part of a growing church is building a building. But how do you know when it is really time to make a huge financial commitment? Do you go into debt or raise the money first? How much do you need to raise before starting to build? As a pastor, I struggled with these questions over and over again.

As Christ followers, we must commit to asking and answering tough questions before we rush in to supporting a new building project. Have we looked at every alternative? What about multiple services, moving our small groups off campus and into homes, or planting a new church? Many of us have approached such projects with the attitude of "we get to build" instead of "we have to build," failing to think about the long-term implications.

If we enter building projects prayerfully, methodically, wisely, and with God's blessing, the end result should be a larger congregation with more capacity to give. Generosity has to be at the core of our values as a church. However, if we enter building projects with the wrong motives, we will not have God's blessing. Debt can easily become an albatross around the very neck of the church.

In the end, we raised the money and built the building. The church continues to thrive and grow. Many people have been saved, lives have been changed, relationships have been restored, and the church is very active in giving and supporting missions. For all intents and purposes, the building campaign was a success. I was a success. But as friends congratulated me on my hard work, my mind was plagued with one thought: *What about those kids in Zhenshi?*

I couldn't escape the reality of what I saw, touched, and smelled in China. Then I stumbled on Proverbs 31:9: "Speak up for the poor and helpless, and see that they get justice." The reality of what I had experienced screamed out one thing: *We're failing. We're failing our children, beloved creations made in God's image. We're failing the body. We're failing the needy. We're failing that orphanage in Zhenshi.*

Let me say clearly that I am not against new or modern buildings. I am not so idealistic to think that every church should meet in houses or old supermarkets. But we have to ask ourselves: Are we investing the majority of our time and energy in the brick and mortar of our buildings while neglecting the biblical command to be the hands and feet of Jesus?

The Budget Issue

Desiring to live out the gospel through adoption, some friends of ours were burdened to welcome Russian orphans into their family. They were thrilled to find a sibling group of two boys and a girl who were waiting to be adopted. It seemed like a clear open door from the Lord.

Much to their dismay, they learned that adopting a sibling group can be exorbitantly expensive because of individual adoption fees for each child, particularly in Russia. But after praying and seeking the Lord, this family felt that God was definitely calling them to adopt these siblings. They were willing to leave their comfortable and stable lives and invite these three needy children (with unknown variables in their lives) into their family.

The biggest obstacle remaining was the money needed to complete the adoption. Our friends approached their pastor to ask if the church would consider helping them. The answer was a quick no. They were told, "We don't give financial help to optional things like adoption."

Optional? Placing orphans in a family is optional? In the pastor's eyes, people adopt only because they want more children. He was not looking at adoption from the perspective of children who desperately need a family, or the perspective of Scripture, which clearly commands the church to care for orphans. There's a big difference.

Many churches are building structures that are controlling them, and they are strangled by debt. It is virtually impossible to care for orphaned and vulnerable children if the majority of our church budgets are gobbled up with mortgage payments. When we are in over our heads in debt, no matter how "spiritual" we are, we are forced to make decisions based on survival. We have to cut the budget somewhere in order to keep the doors open.

Let's be honest: the easiest place to cut a budget is in areas where there are few voices to protest—areas like international mission work and orphan care. If we cut our missions budget, we might get an earful from one or two people who are tied to that particular missionary or agency. In contrast, if we cut the senior adult budget, we risk a local uprising. If we cut the youth budget and stop providing donuts and soft drinks every Sunday morning, you can bet a lot of people will complain.

Too often, it is the "least of these" that are conveniently removed from our budgets. While our programs thrive, children starve. We minister and are ministered to in our oversized, climate-controlled auditoriums, complete with light shows and cutting-edge sound and video technology. Meanwhile, orphans around the world pray for a warm place to sleep at night, for food, for shoes, for a blanket, for clean water . . . for a family.

If someone were to ask your church to sponsor ten children placed in Christian foster homes in Ethiopia, the response might be an easy no. I know this from experience because I have invited many churches to partner with Ethiopian Christians, and the vast majority of them never follow through. "You know," a well-meaning committee member might say, "we just have to be really careful right now and not overextend ourselves with another

$500 a month." But think about it this way. If your church averages 200 people a week in worship, you probably have a budget of at least $200,000 per year. A sponsorship of $500 a month would be 3 percent of your budget.

So where are we spending our money in churches today? According to one recent study, an average of 74 percent of a church's budget goes to cover salaries, utilities, grounds, buildings, maintenance, property insurance, and administration costs. An average of 7 percent is spent on ministries and support, 3 percent goes to denominational contributions and fees, and 6 percent represents "other," which can include anything from repairs to advertising to evangelism and missions. Of that, only 5 percent goes to international missions. In many cases, a large part of international missions offerings covers missionaries' living expenses and overhead costs like buildings, utilities, and upkeep—which is valid and important, but costly.[1]

What does all of this mean for orphaned and vulnerable children? It means that, for many of us, only a trivial amount of the money we put in our offering plates actually reaches the ends of the earth for the child who is starving, freezing to death, suffering from HIV/AIDS, or about to be trafficked.

For the typical church with a budget of $200,000, less than $10,000 a year goes to missions. I'd venture to say that's less than the cumulative amount the families in that average church spend on vacation. Are we missing something? Could we be guilty of building bigger church buildings but failing to truly invest in God's kingdom by caring for orphaned and vulnerable children?

I truly love my church that I used to serve. The people are real, the fellowship is sweet, and their love for Jesus and the gospel cannot, nor should not, be questioned. I am not against innovation, modern buildings, or growing churches. But I do want to clearly communicate this: Despite our passion for the gospel, we are missing something. We must rethink our ministry strategy with orphans in mind. Balance is critical here. We need to take an honest look at how we are spending our money and the motives behind the decisions we are making. Sometimes we will need to repent and change course. Other times we will be able to move forward knowing that we truly have God's blessing. "Build it and they will come" should not be our strategy. Rather, we should ask, "If we build it, can we still do all that God has called us to do?"

Too Smooth for Rough Kids

I am not simply suggesting that church budgets need to change. They do, but that is only part of the solution. Caring for orphaned and vulnerable children is not just about writing a check or sponsoring a child. It starts with the children in our own churches and communities, much like Jesus challenged His disciples to minister, not only to the ends of the earth, but also in Jerusalem (Acts 1:8). It begins with children who have been abused or abandoned, fatherless children, foster children, and adopted children in our nurseries, preschool rooms, children's ministry, and youth groups.

How do you handle the little boy who bites other kids in the nursery? What about the three-year-old who knows words you don't even know? How about the little Chinese girl who is deaf? How do you deal with the seven-year-old boy who is in a wheelchair because his birth mother tried to abort him . . . and failed? What about that fourth grader who was adopted through the foster care system and has profound mental challenges due to an incredibly abusive past? What do you do with the adopted Ethiopian kid who is HIV positive? How do you deal with the special needs toddler who was exposed to drugs in utero? What about that troubled middle schooler who is growing up fatherless?

These are tough questions, and I'm not claiming to have all the answers. But I'm challenging the way we do church, and particularly, the way we approach children's and youth ministry. I cut my teeth in ministry in the 1990s. It was the watermark for the "church growth movement"—a time when many long-standing traditions were questioned and changed to be more welcoming toward newcomers. We debated the style of music, the style of clothes, church service times, coffee in the foyer, perforated communion wafers, and on and on. Books were written, debates held, and some churches were even considered heretical for making these changes.

However, every church agreed on the critical importance of one thing—the nursery and children's departments. At every conference I attended on church growth, I was taught that if your nursery and children's area were not clean, safe, and hazard-free, young families would not come back. As a parent of five children, I totally agree.

But I have to ask this question: Have we gone too far? We want it safe, and that's important. But have we made these areas so sanitary and censored that the "rough" kids aren't welcomed? Jesus spent the majority of His time with people who were rough around the edges—the sick, the outcasts, the poor, the underachievers, the prostitutes, the tax collectors, and the gamblers. He made it very clear that "healthy people don't need a doctor—sick people do" (Matt. 9:12 NLT).

If we desire to truly be the hands and feet of Jesus—not just to build big buildings and sing about how good and loving and faithful God is—we cannot dismiss the difficult kids. We must embrace the children and adolescents who try to "buck" the system, break all the rules, and act out to get attention. We need to make our churches a welcome place for people who need special assistance and care because they are deaf, blind, physically disabled, mentally challenged, or HIV positive.

If we fail to welcome and love these children as Jesus would, we miss God's heart. If we exclude them from our children's ministry programs because it is "too hard" or "too much of a risk," we are turning away the "least of these." How can we sponsor a child in Africa, yet turn away vulnerable children in our own communities?

When we open our arms to love these kids with difficult histories unconditionally, we welcome Jesus. When we go the extra mile by recruiting a sign language interpreter; when we order whatever extra equipment is needed to make sure those who are handicapped can participate; when we see the real person instead of the feeding tube, the wheelchair, or the HIV diagnosis, we love others like God loves them. When we are patient with vulnerable children's emotional and violent outbursts; when we laugh with them, cry with them, and listen to them; and when we welcome children, no matter what they look like, dress like, talk like, or smell like, we allow God's love to shine through us.

In addition, two hours on a Sunday morning at your church might be the only "free time" some parents have during the week. I have to admit, some Sundays my motivation for going to church is not only spiritual, but also because we get free childcare for a few hours. As much as I love my kids, I'm not a "superdad." As parents, Beth and I have the opportunity to receive the blessing of being ministered to through our church. But like many families with special needs children, we have, at times, felt like we are being a burden.

Children's ministries need to go out of their way to support and encourage parents who have kids with special needs. Workers and ministers should welcome these families with open arms, rather than grumbling about "too much extra hassle." At one church we attended, there was a policy requiring all parents to volunteer in the children's department at least once every two months. Fortunately, the staff knew that Beth and I needed a respite on Sunday mornings. We ministered to our children during the week; the church ministered to us on the weekends.

It's one thing to talk big or even give money to an orphanage overseas. But when it comes down to the nitty-gritty—the "rough" kids in our own smooth-running churches—how will we respond?

Churches Are Waking Up

A little boy curled up asleep on the floor of an office cubicle, his only pillow a balled-up coat. That's what changed everything for Bob Coy, pastor of the largest church in Florida. Reading the paper one Sunday morning, he came across this intriguing picture, and he assumed that it was an international report. Bob was shocked when he realized this child lived in his own city of Fort Lauderdale. The boy had been taken into foster care the night before, and there was no home available for him. As a result, he had to sleep in the social worker's office.

Then Bob remembered the voice of the "Pint-Sized Prophet," as he calls her—a little lady in his congregation who had been pestering him for years about getting involved with the foster care system. Bob always thought that it was too messy and too political. He did not want anything to do with government-controlled childcare. He had always taken pride in this well-thought-out answer . . . until now.

As he grabbed his suit coat and headed to church, Bob was struck by the weight of what he had read: *A child in his own community was homeless.* Picking up the paper again later, Bob began to really feel convicted that his church was missing something right under their noses. They had overlooked something critical—something that Jesus cared about.

Pastor Bob began to take a stand for vulnerable children. It wasn't popular. It wasn't easy. But it was right. He was sure of it. It caused quite a bit of a rift when he shared his story with the congregation and announced that the church would be putting the new school building project on hold until something could be put in motion to take care of these children.

Soon, 4KIDS of South Florida was born, a child welfare agency dedicated to meeting the needs of foster children. Their website reads:

> It usually surprises people when they hear it for the first time. We have an orphan problem in America. In our country, the most affluent in the world, we have half a million orphans—children living on the streets, in group homes, and in foster care. South Florida is no exception: Every day, seven kids in South Florida are removed from their homes due to abuse or neglect.
>
> 4KIDS' Vision, "A Home For Every Child in Crisis," speaks to the solvable nature of the problem. It's that simple. If we find a home for a child in crisis, that child finds HOPE. Over 14 years, we've seen this proven again and again though a partnership of committed churches, corporations, foundations, and individuals. Working collectively, we are making a difference one child at a time, and fulfilling our Mission of "Providing Hope . . . For Kids in Crisis."[2]

4KIDS provides crisis support through SafePlace, a temporary location for children who are removed from unsafe home environments. SafePlace is staffed by Christian workers and volunteers from participating churches who provide love and care to kids in crisis. In 2011, more than 800 foster kids found a haven in SafePlace.

In situations where Child Protective Services determines it is not safe for children to return home, 4KIDS works to place children in foster families recruited from local churches. 4KIDS also recruits and trains families to become adoptive parents for foster children who are available for adoption.

Today more than 100 churches participate in 4KIDS, an impact far greater than Pastor Bob could have ever accomplished through just building another building. You see, maybe it is not that churches are dreaming too big with our multiple campuses and high-tech worship services. I daresay we are dreaming too small. We are settling for putting on a show while neglecting the heart of true religion.

When my "orphan conversion" happened in 2005 with James's adoption, I, like Pastor Bob, began to realize the biblical mandate to care for orphaned and vulnerable children. At a luncheon where Steven Curtis Chapman spoke, God began to solidify His calling on my life to challenge the church to care for orphans. And I wanted my church to do something. So, like any good pastor, I got online and decided to order an orphan care ministry kit. I would order the kit, copy the bulletin insert, and go from there. The only problem was that I couldn't find any such kit. I found ministry kits to help churches start a divorce care ministry, a premarital counseling ministry, a singles' ministry, a spiritual seekers' ministry, a quilting ministry, and even a rodeo ministry.

But Google's results were surprisingly short when it came to ministry tools for orphan care, adoption, or foster care. All I found was sponsorship information for organizations like Compassion, World Vision, and World Help. And while that was all well and good, I was convicted to do more than write a check. Needless to say, I was thrilled to get my hands on a prerelease copy of *Starting an Orphan Ministry in Your Church* by Paul Pennington and Jason Weber at Hope for Orphans.

Today, it's a whole different story. You can go online right now and order an orphan care ministry kit.[3] You can sign up to attend national conferences like *The Orphan Summit* or *Together for Adoption*. You can download multiple resources about how your church can support adoption and foster care.

Ministries to orphaned and vulnerable children are sprouting up, not just at Pastor Bob's church but also in many other places around the country. Many Christian families are stepping forward to become foster parents or to adopt. The church is waking up to the biblical mandate to care for orphaned and vulnerable children. "Adoption steps to the front lines of cultural wars," *Christianity Today* asserted in January 2010.[4] It's about time. Orphan care is close to the heart of God, and it should be to us, His followers.

These days, it's becoming "cool" in evangelical circles to be involved in orphan care. As an adoptive father myself, I couldn't be more thrilled. But as excited as I am to see the church mobilized, I have a grave fear: Orphan care may quickly become evangelical America's latest religious fad. Let's not make it just another hip thing to do, another box on the checklist of what it means to be a good Christian, another bumper sticker, or another wristband.

Many churches view orphan care as a "project," but biblically, the church is *the* agent God has set in place for orphan care. As we seek to take seriously God's command to care for orphaned and vulnerable children, let us not fall prey to just buying the T-shirt and joining the movement. We need to make sure that orphan care and adoption are woven into the very DNA and fabric of our churches.

As with any step of obedience, there are new challenges. Adoptions are definitely not all "roses and sunshine." Well-meaning adoptive parents who lack the support of their church community can get to the point of feeling so overwhelmed, discouraged, and alone that they throw in the towel. One family went so far as to place their adopted child on a plane with a one-way ticket back to Russia. In a few extreme cases, parents have even murdered their adopted children. Let's not let it come to that.

Churches are now facing issues that they never thought they would have to face. But we cannot turn a blind eye to these challenges or ignore these desperate needs. We must realize that signing the adoption papers is not the end of the journey; it's just the beginning. Adoptive and foster care families are taking a bold step of faith, but they cannot do it alone.

We Can Do This

It doesn't take a megachurch to make a difference. In 2006, thirty-nine individuals from several Christian organizations met in Little Rock for the very first Orphan Summit. For several days, they prayed and strategized about how God would have them care for orphaned and vulnerable children. That weekend, the Christian Alliance for Orphans (CAFO) was born—a small group of churches and Christian organizations that was proactively seeking to care for orphans. These leaders from Family Life, Focus on the Family, Show Hope, Bethany Christian Services, and other organizations also formed a board of directors to make the Orphan Summit an annual event. Their motto cuts to the heart of the matter: "Leave your ego and logo at the door for the good of the gospel and for children."

Six years later, the Alliance has grown exponentially from its original thirty-nine members to an international movement of concerned Christians and churches. Each year in November, Orphan Sunday brings churches together to "celebrate the love of God who 'places the lonely in families' and calls us to do the same." In 2011 more than 500,000 individuals in the United States were involved in some type of Orphan Sunday activity. More than 100 churches in the Philippines held Orphan Sunday events, and more than 1,000 Eastern European churches honored Orphan Sunday.

Before you think your church is too small to make a difference, you need know that it is not. After all, CAFO started with just thirty-nine people. As a matter of fact, many churches that are the most active and effective in orphan care are not particularly large. City Church Tallahassee in north Florida sponsors ten orphaned children to be placed in Ethiopian foster families instead of living in an orphanage. Orland Park Church in the Chicago area works with an orphanage in Honduras, hosts an Orphan Sunday each year with a dinner that follows, and assembles back-to-school backpacks to provide at-risk and foster children with school supplies and personal dignity.

You can make a difference. But the solutions are much more complex than just building another orphanage or writing out a $30 check every month so a kid can have food. We must learn to think differently, to pray differently, to budget differently, to teach differently, and to live differently. As churches are planted around the world, we can partner with those indigenous churches. The most effective orphan care model always has and always will be local believers ministering to local orphaned children.

But don't act out of guilt or obligation or just because you think it's "cool." Until God breaks your heart for the orphans He loves and longs to rescue, your response will likely be superficial. I challenge you to get on your face before God. Confess and repent of your lack of concern in this area. Ask Him what He would have you do, but only if you're ready to make some radical changes in your life and in your church.

This may involve restructuring your budget, downsizing the building plans, starting an annual Orphan Sunday, and preaching about orphan care, adoption, and related issues. It might include starting an adoption fund to help families adopt, adopting a child yourself, or working with social services to recruit and train members as foster families. Perhaps your church will partner with a church in Ethiopia or Guatemala to help get children out of orphanages and into foster homes, leading to indigenous adoptions. Maybe your church will sponsor children financially so they can continue to live with their own families. You might need to change your children's ministry policies to accommodate at-risk kids in your community, develop a support and discipleship group for teenage moms, or spearhead a sports ministry for kids whose fathers are in jail. And no matter what else you do, encourage your church to put together a team of people to strategize, pray over, and develop the many facets of an orphan care ministry.

The list could go on and on. There are a million ways to get involved. We can do this. We must do this.

What You Can Do

ANYONE can gather a team of people to strategize and pray over how your church can become involved in orphan care and encouraging and supporting adoption. A great way to introduce this ministry to your church is to start an annual Orphan Sunday. A free kit is available at www.adoptionjourney.com/pastorkit.

Many churches now have orphan and adoption ministries, and those teams are very willing to talk with you and share how they have formed their ministries.

MANY can start a ministry in your church that reaches out to families who have adopted children and begin to support and encourage them in tangible and intentional ways. Individual church members can provide childcare one afternoon or evening each week to the family at no cost. This will provide the parents the opportunity to get away and not have to worry about their children. Having consistency helps some of the children with more severe needs develop a greater comfort level with their caregivers.

A FEW can look into and develop a ministry like 4Kids of South Florida. Two other similar ministries are Project 1:27 in Denver, Colorado, and The Call in Little Rock, Arkansas. A FEW can also actually adopt a child with extreme emotional or physical challenges. It will be risky and difficult. Usually the best people to do this are "younger empty nesters"—those who have already raised a few children, know the challenges and have "been there and done that" when it comes to parenting teenagers. You are already seasoned and understand the challenges of parenting. For some of these children, you might be their only hope. Seek God's wisdom as you prayerfully approach opportunities to practice pure and undefiled religion by caring for orphans in distress.

CHAPTER 10

This Is War

Orphans and Spiritual Warfare

Friends, this is war. Satan's great scheme is to destroy the family, and he seems to be doing a pretty good job of it. We must fight back in this spiritual battle.

In recent years, many ministries and churches have invested significant time and energy to strengthen marriages and keep families together, which is a commendable and right thing to do. We have couples' retreats, kids' programs, family camps, parenting classes, financial coaching, and marriage seminars. I would dare say that in almost every city in America, couples in crisis can find a Christian counselor to guide them through the process of rebuilding their relationship.

If a marriage doesn't make it in the church today, it's likely not for a lack of resources or support. As evangelicals, we have given great priority to strengthening marriages because we recognize that Satan's prime target is not the church, the government, or our society at large.

It is the family.

But while we zealously devote ourselves to building up Christian marriages and families, Satan is at work right under our noses with a subtle but deadly strategy—robbing children of the care, protection, and love of their families, leaving them vulnerable to poverty, disease, abuse, and other evils.

The family is God's design for children. In Genesis 1:28, the Lord blesses the family and instructs us to "be fruitful, multiply, fill the earth, and subdue it." God established the family as the foundational institution of His created world—the main context through which the next generation tangibly experiences the Lord's grace, love, discipline, and compassion. This is what Satan most despises and seeks to destroy.

Through our earthly family, God gives us glimpses into the relationship that we have with Him because of the gospel. He is our heavenly Father. As believers, we have been adopted into God's family and given a new name, a new family, and a new future—"But to all who did receive Him, He gave them the right to be children of God" (John 1:12). Over and over in Scripture, the Lord refers to us as His children and He as our Abba Father— our Daddy. As kids, our relationship with God the Father is first understood and shaped by our interactions with our own father.

It is also through the family that real discipleship takes place. God did not instruct youth pastors to bring up their youth group in the nurture and admonition of the Lord; He gave that command to fathers (Eph. 6:4). When it comes to the responsibility of disciplining and shaping the next generation, Scripture speaks directly to parents:

> Love the LORD your God with all your
> heart, with all your soul, and with all your
> strength. These words that I am giving you today
> are to be in your heart. Repeat them to your chil-
> dren. Talk about them when you sit in your house
> and when you walk along the road, when you lie

down and when you get up. Bind them as a sign
on your hand and let them be a symbol on your
forehead. Write them on the doorposts of your
house and on your gates. (Deut. 6:5–9)

If parents are not there to love, instruct, and shape their children, who will be? We must be there for them. We must fight for
them.

The Gospel Come to Life

Twenty-seven hours after leaving China with our new daughter Xiaoli, we finally pulled into our driveway. After weeks of
meetings, paperwork, hotels, and airplanes, home sweet home
was like a dream come true, particularly for Xiaoli, who had no
concept of a home other than her crowded orphanage.

James rushed inside ahead of us and made a beeline to Xiaoli's
bedroom, dragging her in tow. In his broken deaf speech, he
screamed and shouted to his new little sister, "Yours! This yours!
This yours!" Pulling Xiaoli's shoes out of the closet one by one,
James set them carefully in front of her, signing and shouting
"Yours!" all the while. Jerking open her dresser, he began to pile
the clothes around her in mounds, still screaming "Yours!" at the
top of his lungs.

It was quite a sight. Xiaoli was sitting there bewildered—surrounded by shoes, clothes, teddy bears, and toys. Meanwhile,
James was dancing around her room with the sheer joy of a man
who'd just discovered gold. In that moment, James saw something
that the rest of us missed. While Beth and I were preoccupied with
unloading the car and getting dinner on the table, this little boy
understood the radical change that was taking place in Xiaoli's
life.

He had lived it.

As James pulled out Xiaoli's shoes, clothes, and toys, and showed them to her one by one, my son opened my eyes to the gospel. On a very deep level, James understood that his little sister was starting a new life. Far more than just a roof over her head, shoes for her feet, and clothes to put on her back, Xiaoli Carr was now part of a family. She had a new name, a new identity, a new home, and a new future.

The likelihood of Xiaoli spending the rest of her childhood in an orphanage was now 0 percent. The chance of her living in extreme poverty, contracting HIV/AIDS, being trafficked, or bouncing from one foster home to another was now drastically reduced. Xiaoli was welcomed into a family where she would experience unconditional love and support, even if she experienced an unplanned pregnancy one day or faced the evils of racism.

That day, everything changed for Xiaoli. She was not alone anymore.

As James danced around his new sister shouting, "Yours! All yours!" I couldn't help but think of Paul's words to the Corinthian church, "Therefore, if anyone is in Christ, he is a new creation; old things have passed away, and look, new things" (2 Cor. 5:17). Like James, Paul was saying, "It's yours! Everything the gospel has to offer you is yours!"

Our family traveled twenty-seven hours to bring Xiaoli home, but our Redeemer God has journeyed the corridors of history, leaving the glories of heaven for the horrors of the cross, all to bring us home.

The gospel doesn't erase our past, but it drastically changes our future with a living hope. The gospel gives us the opportunity to be healed and to know God as our Abba Father. With our adoption into God's family comes a radically new life. "The Spirit

Himself testifies together with our spirit that we are God's children, and if children, also heirs—heirs of God and coheirs with Christ" (Rom. 8:16–17). As God's children, everything He has is ours. "He did not even spare His own Son but offered Him up for us all; how will He not also with Him grant us everything?" (Rom. 8:32).

Looking back now, I wish I had joined in on James's dancing and shouts of joy—the joy of a man who's discovered "an inheritance that is imperishable, uncorrupted, and unfading, kept in heaven for you" (1 Pet. 1:4).

How Far Are You Willing to Go?

Often, we forget that we were once orphans. Jesus Christ endured the horrors of the cross to rescue us from an eternity in hell. *How far are we willing to go to rescue orphaned children from a living hell?*

Jesus Christ paid with His own blood to adopt us as His children. *What sacrifices are we willing to make to welcome these children into our own families?*

Jesus Christ left the glories of heaven for the sinful stench of this world in order to bring us home. *What are we willing to leave behind in order to make sure that every orphaned and vulnerable child is not alone?*

My brothers and sisters, we have been wrong. We have allowed politics—both government and church politics—to influence and shape us more than the truths of God's Word. We must think about the origins of how we think, how we talk, how we act, how we spend our time and money, and who we do and don't associate with.

We don't want to endanger our reputation, our health, or our lives by reaching out to the homeless or prostitutes in our community in tangible ways, so we avoid those parts of town. We try to avoid "rocking the boat" by bringing up controversial issues, so we fail to address the racism rampant within our church. We are more eager to talk about our new building than the children we are placing in families from orphanages in China. Preoccupied with keeping our families "safe," we forget that many foster children have never experienced the true love of a family.

We frame HIV/AIDS as God's judgment, abdicating ourselves of any responsibility to support education, prevention, or drug treatments. Aiming to send a clear message about sexual purity, we ostracize and make an example of any woman in our congregation who gets pregnant out of wedlock, and many times fail to provide the love and support that she needs. What we don't see is her tearful trip to the abortion clinic and the sleepless nights she endures as a result.

We have all been in situations where we are more concerned about our reputation than about obeying God. We place our own pleasure and comfort above following Christ. But the gospel always calls us out of ourselves and our self-constructed world. It calls us to care, to sacrifice, and to reach out to orphaned and vulnerable children and become the face of Jesus.

Jesus came and died for those with HIV/AIDS, no matter how they got the disease. He died for those living in poverty. He died for the teenager who is selling her body tonight so she doesn't starve. He died for the young woman facing an unplanned pregnancy. He died for every little boy and girl who is orphaned. He died for every angry, confused, and scared boy and girl in foster care whose earthly possessions fit inside one black trash bag.

Not only did Jesus die for these orphaned and vulnerable kids, but He also defeated death, hell, and the grave to rise again. He now offers them the glorious gift of the gospel *through us*.

Counting the Cost

I mentioned earlier that this book was not primarily about adoption, but rather the complex social issues that orphans face every day. However, as you have read these pages, my prayer is that you have come to understand adoption as part of the solution, and I challenge you to seek God's face about adopting a child into your family. But we must also realize that adoption is just one small piece of the puzzle when considering how to best minister to the 153 million orphaned and vulnerable children around the world.

When adoption is the answer, it comes with a unique set of joys and challenges, especially for those adopting older children or those with special needs. Just because we are living out the gospel does not mean God will give us "warm fuzzies." On the contrary, He will more likely give us rowdy little ones who require an extra dose of grace and patience. As an adoptive dad of three, I know firsthand.

If you are considering adoption, you must ask yourself and your family: *Are we willing to pay the price for adoption?* I'm not talking about the adoption fees. I'm talking about you—your time, your emotional energy, your immaculate house, your comfortable life, and your self-absorbed habits. How much did it cost Jesus? Are we really willing to go that far?

Make your own attitude that of Christ Jesus,
who, existing in the form of God, did not consider
equality with God as something to be used for

His own advantage. Instead He emptied Himself
by assuming the form of a slave, taking on the
likeness of men. And when He had come as a man
in His external form, He humbled Himself by
becoming obedient to the point of death—even to
death on a cross. (Phil. 2:5–8)

This is the beautiful, tragic, extreme gospel that has rescued
us. Our God demands all—not only what's easy or comfortable
or safe. He doesn't ultimately want your money. He wants your
heart, emptied of your pride, selfishness, and preoccupation with
"looking good" as you serve.

Jesus emptied Himself. He willingly set aside the discern-
able use of His omnipotence, omnipresence, and omniscience to
become a man. He entered our reality of brokenness, sin, and evil
in order to adopt us. We often overlook this truth with a sugar-
coated view of adoption. If we are going to advocate for adoption
because of what Jesus did for us, we must also be willing to do the
same. We must be willing to humble ourselves to enter a child's
reality of neglect, abuse, malnutrition, emotional/behavioral
problems, and disease. After all, Jesus didn't come to adopt the
"perfect kids"; He welcomed us into His family when we were far
from perfect.

Adoption is not for everyone. Over the past several years, the
landscape of international adoption has drastically changed, and
the majority of adoptable children have physical and/or emotional
challenges. As I've said before, I truly believe there is a family out
there for every child who needs to be adopted, but we must count
the cost.

Jesus came in complete humility so that He could adopt us.
Are we willing to do the same? Are we willing to humble ourselves
to enter into these kids' cultures? Xiaoli has many fond memories

of China, and as much as she is a Carr kid, she will always be Chinese first. Her Chinese heritage is important to her, and we have to make sure it is important to us too. Chinese culture is part of our family—and always will be—because I have a daughter and son who were born Chinese.

We must also humble ourselves to enter into the culture of these children's disabilities, whether it is Down syndrome, Reactive Attachment Disorder, blindness, deafness, or another challenge. Within every disability, there is a unique culture. Since I am the father of three deaf children, it is critical that I take the time and effort to practice signing and learn the nuances of deaf culture. This commitment continually requires humbling myself to ask questions, listen, and learn from others.

With JJ's physical needs, Beth and I feel like we have earned our stripes to be registered nurses. We know all about pulmocort, albuterol, extension tubes, venting, Little Joey feeding pumps, and ankle-foot orthosis. I am doing things for my son that I never thought I would have the ability to do. I never dreamed I'd be a medical technician, but I am because I love my son and he needs to eat through a feeding tube.

I have also seen the change in my oldest son Jared. At twelve years old, he has chosen to take on many of the daily responsibilities of caring for JJ. While his friends are out playing basketball, Jared is giving JJ his medicine through a G-tube. He, too, has earned his RN pin. Jared humbles himself to do things for JJ that most children his age would never dream of doing.

When you open your home to hurting kids, you will likely have to humble yourself as a parent. If you foster a thirteen-year-old who does not have social graces or have any respect for you, it's tough. One of our foster children over the years often had violent outbursts in public places—the grocery store, the mall, the middle of a restaurant—when the slightest thing would set her off.

This child didn't go out of her way to be difficult, but her mental and behavioral challenges were inescapable. As people stared or glared at us, I knew what they were thinking: *They need to learn how to parent a child. Give me five minutes with that kid and I will teach her how to act in public.* Those well-meaning folks had no idea of the trauma this child had experienced. Honestly, we didn't even know the full extent. She looked so "normal" on the outside, but on the inside, the music playing in this little girl's head was foreboding and scary—like the *Jaws* theme. And it played like a broken record.

Finally, you will have to humble yourself to enter these children's pain. This may be the hardest area for many of us. We are limited in how much of the hurt we can remove. Sometimes all we can do is hold our child tight, catch the tears as they fall, and cry out to God to heal.

I'll never forget the night that nine-year-old James walked into the kitchen with a troubled look on his face. He and Xiaoli are different when it comes to their past—she often talks about her memories of China, but James rarely wants to. After four years of being home with us—four years of safety, love, and consistent care—James finally signed the question that plagued his heart: "Why did my momma leave me on the road?"

Then the tears flowed. Beth and I tried to talk with him, but we soon realized that our little boy didn't need words. He didn't really need an "answer." James needed us to enter into his pain with him. For forty-five minutes, he and I sat on the sofa together. I held him in my arms and we both cried. We cried over what James had lost and what he'd never know. We cried because we live in a fallen, sinful world and sometimes things just don't make sense. And I like to think that Jesus was right there, crying with us, too. Because wherever there is brokenness and pain, our

Redeemer God weeps with us, and only He can heal the wounds of James's heart.

Not By Our Own Strength

"It's too tough," you might say. "I could never go through that."

You're right. But I challenge you: All along, God has been waiting for you to acknowledge this truth. In your own strength, you can't do it. So let's dig deeper into the apostle Paul's words to the Philippians: "For it is God who is working in you, enabling you both to desire and to work out *His* good purpose" (Phil. 2:13, emphasis added). This is the crux of orphan care and adoption—it is not by our strength, wisdom, or knowledge alone that we parent well. Will we use these skills? Of course. God has gifted each one of us, entrusted us with talents, and given us minds to think. But it is God who works in us "for His purpose." With Him, all things really are possible—including parenting a child that comes from a very hard place.

Orphan care is far more than a humanitarian effort or an issue of social justice. This is war. When you care for orphaned and vulnerable children, when you work to reverse this vicious cycle that Satan has so masterfully orchestrated, you are fighting against the devil himself. "For our battle is not against flesh and blood, but against the rulers, against the authorities, against the world powers of this darkness, against the spiritual forces of evil in the heavens" (Eph. 6:12).

Ultimately, orphan care is a gospel issue. It's about Jesus Christ and His work. And the amazing irony is that as we live out the gospel to these hurting kids, we also experience the gospel in ways we never imagined.

As we gird ourselves for battle, we must be mindful of a few things. First, we must not settle for cheap solutions to the social issues of our day related to orphan care and adoption. We must also recognize that our battle is not against liberals or conservatives, governments or political parties—not even those with different religious beliefs. This is a battle that has already been won through the shed blood, death, and resurrection of Jesus Christ.

The gospel wins. But the gospel is applied through believers. We can no longer be silent. God is beckoning His people to set aside our pride, selfishness, and lack of concern, and take up the gospel. He desires for us to raise a battle cry on behalf of these forgotten children, to fight for their futures, and to welcome some of them into our families.

It is imperative that we fast and pray about all aspects of orphan care. We must pray for the orphans themselves. We need to go before God as we fight against the injustices that orphans face. We must lift up families in the adoption process, as well as adopted or foster families who are having a difficult time in the transition of their child into the home. These families need not only physical and emotional help, they also need real spiritual breakthroughs—the kind that comes from fasting and prayer. All of us must ask God to show us the specific ways He wants us to help the orphaned and vulnerable children in our world.

When we realize the fact that spiritual warfare is at the heart of the orphan crisis, it brings prayer to a whole new level. It is desperately needed and extremely important.

A Radical Life

When we found James, Xiaoli, and JJ, our family had no idea of the radical changes we would experience together. Through this journey, I have come to understand the gospel and the love of my heavenly Father like never before. I have found a life that I never knew existed—not a job or a ministry, but a life of compassion and action, becoming a voice for the voiceless.

Each day, as I watch our adopted children grow and thrive, I more deeply grasp the truth of James 1:27: "Pure and undefiled religion before our God and Father is this: To look after orphans and widows in their distress and to keep oneself unstained by the world."

Notes

Introduction

1. Childinfo: Monitoring the Situation of Children and Women, "Orphan Estimates," http://www.childinfo.org/hiv_aids_orphanestimates.php.

2. ChildStats.gov, "POP1 Child Population: Number of Children (in millions) Ages 0–17 in the United States by Age," http://www.childstats.gov/americaschildren/tables/pop1.asp.

Chapter 1

1. Zhenshi is not a real city in China. It translates "real China." To protect our friends' work, we have chosen not to disclose the actual cities from which our children were adopted.

2. Marcia E. Herman-Giddens, Jamie B. Smith, Manjoo Mittal, Mandie Carlson, and John D. Butts, "Newborns Killed or Left to Die by a Parent: A Population-Based Study," *The Journal of the American Medical Association* 289, no. 11 (2003): 1425–29.

3. E. J. Graff, "The Lie We Love," *Foreign Policy,* November–December 2008, 59.

4. U.S. Department of Health and Human Services, "Foster Care Statistics 2010," May 2012, Child Welfare Information Gateway, http://www.childwelfare.gov/pubs/factsheets/foster.cfm.

5. Personal communication with Pamela Harrington, February 2012.

6. Alvin Schmidt, *How Christianity Changed the World* (Grand Rapids: Zondervan, 2004), 130.

Chapter 2

1. International Labour Organization, "ILO 2012 Global Estimate of Forced Labour Executive Summary," http://www.ilo.org/washington/WCMS_181953/lang--en/index.htm.

2. International Justice Mission, "Sex Trafficking Fact Sheet," 2010, http://www.ijm.org/sites/default/files/resources/Factsheet-Sex-Trafficking.pdf.

3. Ibid.

4. Muhammad Saad Khan, "Human Trafficking Around the World: The Global Reach of Modern-Day Slavery," CMV Live, January 24, 2012, http://cmvlive.com/local-news/human-trafficking-around-the-world-the-global-reach-of-modern-day-slavery.

5. Dina Francesa Haynes, "Used, Abused, Arrested and Deported: Extending Immigration Benefits to Protect the Victims of Trafficking and to Secure the Prosecution of Traffickers," Human Rights Quarterly 26 (2004): 227.

6. United Nations, "United Nations General Assembly to Focus on International Efforts to Combat Human Trafficking at Headquarters 3 June," Press Release, http://www.un.org/News/Press/docs/2008/note6152.doc.htm.

7. U.S. Department of State, "Trafficking in Persons Report," 2009.

8. International Crisis Aid, "Sex Trafficking in the United States," http://www.crisisaid.org/ICAPDF/Trafficking/traffickstats.pdf.

9. Reshma Kirpalani and Christina Ng, "Missouri Couple Silent on Order to Return Adopted Daughter to Guatemala," ABC News Online, August 5, 2011, http://abcnews.go.com.

10. Huma Khan, "Child Sex Trafficking Growing in the U.S.: 'I Got My Childhood Taken from Me,'" ABC News Online, May 5, 2010, http://abcnews.go.com.

11. Elissa Cooper, "Sexual Slavery on Main Street," *Christianity Today* Online, April 30, 2010, http://www.christianitytoday.com/ct/2010/may/5.17.html?paging=off.

12. Shared Hope, "Take the Pledge," http://www.sharedhope.org/thedefenders.

13. See International Justice Mission, http://www.ijm.org.

14. See Run For Their Lives, http://www.r4tl.org.

15. Matthew Barnett, *The Church That Never Sleeps* (Nashville: Thomas Nelson, 2000), 99.

16. See http://www.streetgrace.org.

Chapter 3

1. USAID, "USAID Country Health Statistical Report: Ethiopia," May 2009, http://pdf.usaid.gov/pdf_docs/PNADO684.pdf.

2. Childinfo, "Orphan Estimates," http://www.childinfo.org/hiv_aids_orphanestimates.php.

3. UNAIDS, "Nearly 50% of People Who are Eligible for Antiretroviral Therapy Now Have Access to Lifesaving Treatment," Press Release, http://www.unaids.org.

4. Childinfo: Monitoring the Situation of Children and Women, "Estimated Numbers of People Living with HIV and HIV Prevalence," http://www.childinfo.org/hiv_aids_estimated.php.

5. UPI, "Homosexuals Found Particularly Liable to Common Viruses," *New York Times,* December 10, 1981, retrieved from http://www.nytimes.com/1981/12/10/us/homesexuals-found-particularly-liable-to-common-viruses.html.

6. John Piper, "Guilt, Grace, and the Global AIDS Crisis," Desiring God Online, http://www.desiringgod.org.

7. *Christianity Today* Online, "Close Encounters with HIV," Editorial, February 1, 2006, http://www.christianitytoday.com/ct/2006/february/17.30.html?paging=off.

8. AVERT Online, "Women, HIV, and AIDS," http://www.avert.org/women-hiv-aids.htm.

9. Russell D. Moore, "Jesus Has AIDS," December 1, 2011, http://www.russellmoore.com/2011/12/01/jesus-has-aids-2.

10. Personal conversation with Elizabeth Styffe, November 28, 2007, at Saddleback Church.

11. World AIDS Orphans Day, "The Facts," http://www.worldaidsorphans.org/section/the_orphans_crisis/the_facts.

12. Ibid.

13. Sarah Eekhoff Zylstra, "No Child Left to Die," *Christianity Today* Online, November 29, 2010, http://www.christianitytoday.com/ct/2010/december/3.17.html?start=1.

14. Mary Katherine Keown, "Female Genital Mutilation Linked to AIDS," *Toronto Star* Online, http://www.thestar.com/living/Health/article/250720.

15. CBC News Online, "Haiti Raises Quake Death Toll on Anniversary," January 12, 2011, http://www.cbc.ca/news/world/story/2011/01/12/haiti-anniversary-memorials.html.

16. For more information or to download this HIV Toolkit, visit http://www.bethany.org/main/hiv-toolkit.

17. Uwe Siemon-Netto, "The Church's Response to AIDS," *Worldwide Religious News* Online, February 20, 2002, http://wwrn.org/articles/4226/?&section=health-medical.

18. HIV&AIDS Initiative Online, "What We Do: The CHURCH Strategy," http://hivaidsinitiative.com/initiative/whatwedo.

19. For more information about the Mille and Medicine Program in Zambia, visit http://www.bethany.org/Main/Zambia.

Chapter 4

1. Andrew Heavens, "Ethiopian President and Olympic Stars Launch 'Dream Campaign' for Orphaned Children," UNICEF Online, November 7, 2006, http://www.unicef.org/infobycountry/ethiopia_36492.html.

2. United Nations, "18,000 Children Die Every Day of Hunger, UN Says," *USA Today* Online, February 17, 2007, http://www.usatoday.com/news/world/2007-02-17-un-hunger_x.htm.

3. Alvin Schmidt, *How Christianity Changed the World* (Grand Rapids, MI: Zondervan, 2004), 132.

4. Robert Broderick, *Catholic Encyclopedia* (Nashville: Thomas Nelson, 1990), 323.

5. Schmidt, *How Christianity Changed the World*, 130.

6. Alan Philips and John Lahutsky, *The Boy from Baby House 10: From the Nightmare of a Russian Orphanage to a New Life in America* (New York: St. Martin's Press, 2009).

7. Judith Norman and Zita Bathori-Tartsi, "Improvisational International Research: Seeking to Help Ukrainian Orphanages Sooner than Later," *Families in Society* 91, no. 4 (October–December 2010): 421.

8. Ibid., 421.

9. Andrea Freidus, "Raising Malawi's Children: Unanticipated Outcomes Associated with Institutionalized Care," *Children and Society* 24, no. 4 (June 2010): 293–303.

10. B. N. Olson and A. B. Kholmogrova, "The Professional Foster Family as One Model for Solving the Orhan Problem in Russia," *Russian Education and Society* 45, no. 6 (June 2003): 26–44.

11. Marinus van IJzendoorn, Maarteje PCM Luijk, and Femmie Juffer, "IQ of Children Growing up in Children's Homes: A Meta-Analysis." *Merrill-Palmer Quarterly* 54, no. 3 (July 2007): 341–66.

12. O. K. Caman and H. Ozcebe, "Adolescents Living in Orphanages in Ankara: Psychological Symptoms, Level of Physical Activity, and Associated Factors," *Turkish Journal of Psychiatry* 22, no. 1 (Spring 2011).

13. C. J. Groak, R. B. McCall, and L. Fish, "Characteristics of Environments, Caregivers, and Children in Three Central American Orphanages," *Infant Mental Health Journal* 32, no. 2 (March–April 2011): 232–50.

14. J. Bowlby, *Maternal Care and Mental Health* (Geneva: World Health Organization, 1951).

15. Z. Simsek, P. N. Erol, D. Oztop, and O. Ozer Ozcan, "Epidemiology of Emotional and Behavioral Problems in Children and Adolescents Reared in Orphanages: A National Comparatives Study," *Turkish Journal of Psychiatry* 19, no. 3 (Fall 2008): 235–46.

16. Celia W. Dugger, "Aid Gives Alternative to African Orphanages," *New York Times* Online, December 7, 2009, http://www.nytimes.com/2009/12/06/world/africa/06orphans.html; "Orphanages: The Myths and Reality of Institutional Care," *Children's Rights,* 2008, http://poundpuplegacy.org/node/17680; National Coalition for Child Protection Reform, "Just Say No to the Orphanage," http://www.nccpr.org/reports/15Orphanage.pdf; Shelley Thiele, "Exploring the Feasibility of Foster Care as a Primary Permanency Option for Orphans," *University of South Africa*, August 5, 2009, http://hdl.handle.net/10500/927; A. M. Tomison and J. Stanley, "Strategic Directions in Child Protection: Informing Policy and Practice," South Australian Department of Human Services, http://aifs. gov.au/nch/pubs/reports/SAbrief/SAbrief5.pdf; K. Davis, "New Models for Orphan Care," *Associate Baptist Press,* July 20, 2010, http://www.abpnews.com/content/view/5355/53/; L. Blerk, "Alternative Care Giving in the Context of AIDS in Southern Africa: Complex Strategies for Care," *Journal of International Development,* December 19, 2006, http://onlinelibrary.wiley.com/doi/10.1002/jid.1328/abstract; J. J. Sigal, J. C. Perry, M. Rossingnol, and M. C. Ouimet, "Unwanted Infants: Psychological and Physical Consequences of Orphanage Care 50 Years Later," *American Journal of Orthopsychiatry* 73, no. 1 (January 2003): 3–12.

17. UNICEF, "Rwanda: Facts and Figures," http://www.unicef.org/infobycountry/23867_20292.html.

18. Bahoneza Online, "Prime Minister Calls upon Rwandans to End Orphanage," January 5, 2012, http://bahoneza.com/2012/01/prime-minister-calls-upon-rwandans-to-end-orphanage.

Chapter 5

1. World Hunger Education Service, "2012 World Hunger and Poverty Facts and Statistics," http://www.worldhunger.org/articles/learn/world%20hunger%20facts%202002.htm.
2. National Center for Children in Poverty, "Child Poverty," http://www.nccp.org/topics/childpoverty.html.
3. Ruby K. Payne, *A Framework for Understanding Poverty,* Updated Edition (Highlands, TX: aha! Process, Inc., 2005), 5.
4. Ibid., 8.
5. Martin Luther, "The Last Written Words of Luther," February 16, 1546, http://www.iclnet.org/pub/resources/text/wittenberg/luther/beggars.txt.
6. Wess Stafford, *Too Small to Ignore: Why the Least of These Matters Most* (Colorado Springs: Waterbrook, 2007), 47.

Chapter 6

1. U.S. Department of Health and Human Services, "The AFCARS Report: Preliminary FY 2010 Estimates as of June 2011," http://www.acf.hhs.gov/programs/cb/stats_research/afcars/tar/report18.htm.
2. Ibid.
3. U.S. Department of Health and Human Services, "Foster Care Statistics 2010," http://www.childwelfare.gov/pubs/factsheets/foster.pdf#Page=1&view=Fit.
4. Ibid.
5. Ibid.
6. Karyn Purvis, David Cross, and Wendy Sunshine, *The Connected Child: Bring Hope and Healing to Your Adoptive Family* (New York: McGraw-Hill, 2007).
7. Ibid.
8. James C. Dobson, *The Strong-Willed Child,* (Carol Stream, IL: Tyndale, 1978), 164.
9. U.S. Department of Health and Human Services, "Foster Care Statistics 2010."
10. U.S. Department of Health and Human Services, "The AFCARS Reports: Preliminary FY 2010 Estimates as of June 2011,"

http://www.acf.hhs.gov/programs/cb/stats_research/afcars/tar/report18.
htm.

11. C. S. Lewis, *The Four Loves* (Orlando, FL: Harcourt Brace,
1960), 169.

12. Russell D. Moore, *Adopted for Life: The Priority of Adoption
for Christian Families & Churches* (Wheaton, IL: Crossway, 2009);
Richard D. Phillips, *Reclaiming Adoption: Missional Living by the
Rediscovery of Abba Father* (CreateSpace.com, 2010); Daniel J.
Bennett, *A Passion for the Fatherless: Developing a God-Centered
Ministry to Orphans* (Grand Rapids: Kregel, 2011); Tony Merida and
Rick Morton, *Orphanology: Awakening to Gospel-Centered Adoption
and Orphan Care* (Birmingham: New Hope Publishers, 2011).

Chapter 7

1. ABC News, "Kentucky Church Bans Interracial Couples,"
December 1, 2011, http://www.abcnews.go.com/US/Kentucky-church-
bans-interracial-couples/story?id=15065204#.UOhRnOTOOn9.

2. "Black Couple Not Allowed to Wed at Mississippi Church," *Fox
25*, July 30, 2012, http://www.okcfox.com/newsroom/top_stories/vid-
eos/kokh_vid_5808.shtml.

3. Billy Graham, as cited in *War Cry of the Salvation Army* 113
(1993): 3.

Chapter 8

1. Susan Donaldson James, "Down Syndrome Births Are Down in
U.S.," ABC News Online, November 2, 2009, http://abcnews.go.com/
Health/w_ParentingResource/down-syndrome-births-drop-us-women-
abort/story?id=8960803.

2. Ibid.

3. The abortion clinic is no longer there. While we were final-
izing this book, the clinic was destroyed by fire in 2012. The clinic
was demolished by order of the city because the damage was so severe.
They have relocated and continue to be in business.

4. Peter Carlson, "A Holy War in Pensacola," *People* Online,
January 21, 1985, http://www.people.com/people/archive/arti-
cle/0,,20089732,00.html.

5. Heather Koerner, "Christian Women Having Abortions,"
Boundless Online, January 24, 2008, www.boundlessline.org/2008/01/
christian-women.html.

6. Lawrence Finer, et. al, "Reasons U.S. Women Have Abortions: Quantitative and Qualitative Perspectives," *Perspectives on Sexual and Reproductive Health* 37, no. 3 (September 2005): 110.

7. Sarah Kliff, "About 40 Percent of Women Have Had Abortions: The Math Behind the Stat," *The Daily Beast*, March 4, 2010, http://www.thedailybeast.com.

8. Rachel Jones, Lawrence Finer, and Susheela Singh, "Characteristics of U.S. Abortion Patients, 2008," Gutt Macher Institutek May 2010, http://www/guttmacher.org/pubs/US-Abortion-Patients.pdf.

9. Jason DeParle and Sabrina Tavernise, "The New Normal: A Child Out of Wedlock," *New York Times*, February 18, 2012, http://www.msnbc.msn.com/id/46438194/ns/us_news-the_new_york_times/t/new-normal-child-out-wedlock.

10. Southern Baptist Convention, "Position Statements: Sanctity of Human Life," http://sbc.net/aboutus/pssanctity.asp.

11. *The Boston Globe* Online, "Memorable lines from Barney Frank," November 28, 2011, http://www.bostonglobe.com.

12. Mike Huckabee, *Do the Right Thing: Inside the Movement That's Bringing Common Sense Back to America* (New York: Penguin Group, 2009), 37.

13. CNN Newsroom, "Bringing the Presidential Candidates Unfiltered, Up Close and in Their Own Words. Speeches by Republican Mike Huckabee, Democrat John Edwards, and Republican John McCain." *CNN* Online, January 13, 2008, http://transcripts.cnn.com/TRANSCRIPTS/0801/13/cnr.02.html.

14. *The Boston Globe* Online, "Memorable lines from Barney Frank," November 28, 2011, http://www.bostonglobe.com.

15. The National Campaign to Prevent Teen and Unplanned Pregnancy, "Fast Facts," April 2009, http://www.thenationalcampaign.org/resources/pdf/FastFacts_DirectCosts_UnplPreg.pdf.

16. National Right to Life, "Abortion Statistics," January 2011, http://www.nrlc.org/Factsheets/FS03_AbortionInTheUS.pdf.

17. Megan Lindsey, "*Adoption Advocate* No. 43: 2012 Policy Priorities and Adoption-Related Legislation," January 2012, https://www.adoptioncouncil.org/publications/adoption-advocate-no-43.html.

Chapter 9

1. NationalChristianPoll.com, "Church Budget Priorities Survey Executive Report," 2009, http://blogs.lifeway.com/blog/domoreministry/npsEE9.tmp.pdf.

2. 4KIDS of South Florida Online, "About Us," http://www.4kidsofsfl.org/about4KIDS.

3. The Christian Alliance for Orphans at http://www.christianalliancefororphans.org is one of many great resources.

4. Bobby Ross, "Orphans on Deck," *Christianity Today,* January 2010, http://www.christianitytoday.com/ct/2010/january/7.12.html.

SERVING GOD BY CARING FOR CHILDREN

For 67 years, Bethany has responded with compassion, integrity, and commitment to children and families in need. Globally, millions are orphaned or abandoned due to poverty. Bethany helps families stay together by providing social services and assistance. We preserve life through pregnancy counseling, and we find families for children in need through adoption.

You can help!

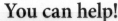